the strategically small church

the strategically small church

Brandon J. O'Brien

BETHANYHOUSE

MINNEAPOLIS, MINNESOTA

Published by Bethany House Publishers
11400 Hampshire Avenue South
Bloomington, Minnesota 55438

Bethany House Publishers is a division of
Baker Publishing Group, Grand Rapids, Michigan.

Printed in the United States of America

In keeping with biblical principles of creation stewardship, Baker Publishing Group advocates the responsible use of our natural resources. As a member of the Green Press Initiative, our company uses recycled paper when possible. The text paper of this book is comprised of 30% post-consumer waste.

Library of Congress Cataloging-in-Publication Data

O'Brien, Brandon J.
    The strategically small church : intimate, nimble, authentic, effective / Brandon J. O'Brien.
        p. cm.
    Includes bibliographical references.
    Summary: "A former pastor and journalist explores the strategic advantages of small churches, explaining how they can sometimes reach their communities more effectively than big churches can"—Provided by publisher.
    ISBN 978-0-7642-0783-9 (pbk. : alk. paper) 1. Small churches. I. Title.
    BV637.8.O27   2010
    253—dc22

                                                        2010004350

For Amy, a gracious partner and passionate minister of the gospel. And for Anchor Baptist Church, the best small church I've yet had the pleasure to know.

Contents

I pastor a small church that we planted nine years ago. I love our congregation and what God is doing through it. So why is it I feel insecure every time someone asks me how many people attend our church? Why do I think the success of my church plant is going to be judged by the number of congregants we have? And why do I feel the urge to report higher numbers? If you pastor a small church, be honest, you struggle with the same thoughts.

A couple of years ago, I attended a large pastor's conference close to my home in Orange County. The speakers were amazing, the program exciting, and the energy contagious. On many levels it was inspiring, but something about it made me uneasy. On my second day at the conference, I realized what it was: Every one of the speakers on the big stage pastored a mega-church of thousands. Yet the vast majority of the pastors in attendance were at churches of less than five hundred. How do I know? Because these are the facts. According to the Hartford Institute for Religion Research, 94 percent of all existing churches have less than five hundred attendees, and two-thirds of these have less than one hundred. Churches of more than two thousand attendees represent less than one half of one percent of all churches in America. As I sat at the conference, I wondered why we hold these mega-churches up as the model of ministry for every church. Is it because, I asked myself, they are large and "successful"? Yet if the majority of pastors are serving at small churches and these conferences are meant to equip and encourage these pastors, why are there no small-church pastors up on the big stage who can teach us what it means to be a small-church pastor? Certainly there are some amazing leaders and teachers at small churches. Could it be because we have bought into the notion that small churches are failed churches and they can only become successful if they follow a certain plan and grow to a certain size? Why have we allowed the ministry experience of one half of one percent of all churches to become the standard by which we judge the remaining 99.5 percent of churches?

What if we saw reality differently? What if God's plan for most churches is to be small? What if the best model for the church is to stay under five hundred people, and even closer to the tipping point of one hundred fifty? Could it be that we have hundreds of thousands of insecure, depressed small-church pastors who have no reason to feel inadequate? And if we changed our perspective, dreamed a different dream, what difference would it make, not just for the psyche of the pastors in America but for the advancement of God's kingdom purposes?

This is the dream that Brandon O'Brien has dared to dream. He is out to change the perception that small churches have failed models of ministry. Never does he say that all small churches are healthy just because of their size. They may not be. But what he does in these pages is show that small churches have amazing strategic advantages. In fact, in six different areas—evangelism, authenticity, leanness, discipleship, intergenerational ministry, and leadership training—the strategically small church has huge advantages over the large church. Does this surprise you?

As Brandon covers each of these topics he is involved in the exercise of changing perceptions. And I found my perspective shifting as I read. I felt less trapped in the "narrative of obscurity" that is the birthright of small-church pastors. I became more emboldened and confident that I am part of a missional movement of churches that is changing the world in the global South and someday in this country, as well. It is my hope that small-church pastors, leaders, and members will read this book and stop wasting valuable energy trying to imitate large-church ministry, and instead recognize the inherent and strategic strengths of small churches. This means getting excited about what God is doing and plans to do through your church. Read this book and be inspired. I was.

—Jim Belcher, author of *Deep Church*

The title of this book may require some explanation. No doubt the words *strategically* and *small* mean different things to different people. And when you put the words together—*strategically small*—they may not mean anything to anyone. (To make matters worse, the definition of the word *church* has been up for debate in recent years, too. I don't intend to wander into that minefield.) But if you'll humor me for just a few paragraphs, I hope to tell you what this book is about and why you should read it.

Let me start by telling you what I *don't* mean when I use the word *strategically*. I don't mean to imply that this book will offer you strategies and methods for helping your small church become large. There are plenty of those sorts of books on the market, and I wouldn't be qualified to write one if I wanted to. In other words, I am not assuming in this book that the local church's primary goal is to grow in numbers.

On the other hand, I also do not mean to offer strategies and methods to help you keep your church from growing. *Strategically small* does not mean "intentionally small." You will meet a few pastors and churches in these chapters who feel called to plant many small churches rather than growing a single large one. But they are in the minority. There are many books on the market today that suggest churches should be kept small so they can remain faithful to their mission, that being large is necessarily bad. This is not one of those books.

You might think that the word *small* is self-explanatory. I thought the same thing not long ago. But I've found after talking to pastors around the country and researching small churches in America that there is great disagreement over what makes for a small congregation. It turns out pastors will compete over anything. Tell a minister about a church of 150, and he just might say, "That's not a small church. There are only twenty-five people in my congregation. Now *that's* a small church."

For our purposes in this book, I've chosen to define *small* broadly. I tell stories from my own experience as a pastor in very small congregations. The smallest was made up of a single family, about six people, and the largest had about 100 members at its high point. The church I served the longest had around twenty in regular attendance. But I also tell stories of congregations with 200 or more members. With only one exception that I know of, every church I highlight has fewer than 300 regular attendees. The overwhelming majority of churches in America have fewer than 500 attendees (more on this in the next chapter). Over half have fewer than 300. And while I know that a church of 300 faces very different challenges than a church of fifty, I believe the contents of this book are applicable to nearly every congregation, and I don't want to exclude anyone from reading it on the basis of size.

More abstractly, *small* can be a state of mind as much as a description of size. In my mind, small churches are ones that are painfully aware of their limitations. They see families leave because they cannot provide attractive programming for children and youth. They may not baptize many new believers, and they assume this is because they can't produce a professional quality worship experience. In short, they operate from a strong sense of what they lack.

I still haven't answered your question directly: What *is* a strategically small church? A strategically small church is one that has become comfortable being small, because it has learned to recognize the unique advantages of its size. A strategically small church realizes it can accomplish things that larger churches cannot. This doesn't make it better or godlier. But it means it can proceed in ministry not from a sense of its deficiencies, but from confidence in its strengths. Strategically small churches are strategic for the kingdom of God, because when they embrace their identity, they can make an enormous impact.

That definition may still seem a bit vague, but that's sort of the point. Nowhere in this book do I try to prescribe steps or procedures for becoming strategically small. Instead I tell stories of how other churches have leveraged their strengths in order to become more effective in their ministries. My job has been to make these stories as compelling as possible so that they inspire you with a vision of what small church ministry can look like. Your job as you read is to determine which of these ideas you can incorporate into your own ministries, and which ones don't make sense in your context. I've written with a deep conviction that every church is unique, because every church member is individually gifted by the Holy Spirit and every congregation does ministry in a different culture and context. So I'd rather offer you illustrations of strategically small ministry than to make up a textbook definition. The hard work of application is yours to undertake.

With that being said, here are a few categories of churches that I consider strategically small. You'll hear more about these churches in the chapters that follow. A strategically small church may be:

- A small church that has recognized the unique benefits of being small and is leveraging those benefits for an effective ministry to its congregation and surrounding community. This is the most common category, and the one this book is most intended to address.

- A large church that has begun to recognize its size as a liability. As a result, the leadership tries to channel the strengths of small churches in its own ministries.

- A church of any size that plants and grows and plants again in an effort to deliberately maintain a network of small (usually fewer than 300 members) congregations. They do this because they recognize small size as more effective than large size for things like evangelism, leadership development, and spiritual formation.

In short, the strategically small church has come to see the supposed liabilities of being small as hidden advantages. And they are learning how to put those advantages to work.

A Little About Myself

It may be important to you to know about the person whose book you're reading. As I mentioned above, I have served in vocational ministry. My wife serves as minister of Christian education at our relatively small church (around 300 in regular attendance) in a western suburb of Chicago. As a spouse of a church leader, I'm more aware than I'd like to be of the daily pressures and challenges pastors, elders, and layleaders face in smaller churches. In other words, I come to this subject with a little experience and a lot of sympathy.

Perhaps more important, I am writing as an editor for *Leadership* journal. During my time in that role, I've had the privilege of traveling the country to meet with pastors of churches of all sizes, attend conferences, visit worship services, and read and edit articles from pastors hoping to encourage their fellow-laborers in the gospel. We hear a lot in the media about what is wrong with American churches, and no doubt there is plenty to criticize. But my role as an intimate observer of American Christianity and a friend of pastors has given me ample opportunity to see all that is right with the church in the United States, as well. Seeing these great churches, most of them small, make a lasting impact in their communities and in the lives of parents and young people, has been an incomparable blessing. But because we are often distracted by what the largest of churches are doing, the stories of smaller churches go untold. This book tells those stories, and I trust they will encourage you as profoundly as they have encouraged me.

Finally, I am a doctoral student in American Christianity. There are a few—very few—historical anecdotes in this book that I hope have made it richer. More than anything, I think historical study provides perspective. My personal study has helped me understand the contemporary church more clearly. I hope the few historical insights in these pages will do the same for you.

Who Is This Book For?

This book is intended for a broad audience. I hope it will be of use to pastors in established traditional churches, church planters looking for a new vision of ministry success, and folks like me who feel called to ministry in the local church but haven't yet found their place. The churches I highlight in these chapters minister in urban, suburban, and rural contexts. They represent an assortment of denominational affiliations and leadership styles and methodologies. What they all have in common is a commitment to helping their church members grow deeper in their commitment to the gospel of Jesus Christ and a passion to carry that gospel into their communities. If you share those qualities, this book is for you.

I want to make it clear that this book advocates for traditional ministry. There are many books on the market today that endorse something like strategically small ministry but are written by proponents of the house church movement or what is called the organic church movement. These perspectives generally advocate for nontraditional meeting places, such as homes, coffeehouses, or anywhere a handful of disciples can meet to study the Scriptures and encourage and edify one another. Moreover, they tend to downplay the significance of paid professional clergy in favor of a more democratic form of church leadership. In other words, they are promoting legitimate expressions of "church," but not as most of us know and experience it. I personally know several pastors and writers in these movements, and I have a great deal of respect for their vision. But this book is for the rest of us—those who value corporate worship services, may meet in a church building, and are led by a paid pastor or elder.

Just One More Thing

Allow me to offer one final word to clarify the purpose of this book. Small church pastor and advocate Chuck Warnock says that small churches are "in definite need of brand revival." The term *brand* refers to the set of experiences and associations consumers connect with a particular product. Good branding is what makes people pay $50 for a shirt that costs $10 to make. Bad branding, on the other hand, keeps people from buying a product no matter what it costs or how good it is. The small church, Warnock believes, has been saddled with a bad brand. Among the unfavorable impressions associated with the small church, Warnock fears people view it as stuck in the past with no vision for the future, unwilling to grow, and lacking the resources to do real ministry—in other words, dead, dull, and boring.

I'm afraid he's right. My goal in this book is to spark

something like a brand revival for small churches. I hope that after reading this book you will see the smaller congregation in more positive terms—as intimate, authentic, nimble, empowering, vibrant, and effective. I hope you'll see that what makes some small churches ineffective is not their size. The problem is the pastor's and/or congregants' perception of success. If we alter our perceptions, we might find we have everything we need. But I'm jumping ahead of myself. For more on that, turn the page.

Chapter One

See for Yourself:
Reimagining Ministry Success

In September 1540, Spanish conquistador Garcia López de Cárdenas and a handful of his comrades happened upon something no other European had ever seen before: the Grand Canyon. It's difficult to imagine what they must have felt. López didn't keep a journal or record his experience in a travel log. We only know that he hurried back from the edge of that deep chasm as soon as he saw it, gripped with awe that was almost painful to behold.

Novelist Walker Percy (1916–1990) believed that López was not only the first European to see the Canyon, he was nearly the last to see it in its original state, with no prior expectations. This is because the explorer—tired and thirsty after a twenty-day march across the Colorado plateau—stumbled upon the gorge. He was just trudging along, and there it was.

As for the rest of us, our experience of the Grand Canyon is determined by our expectations. Popular culture has immortalized the iconic road trip out West, which invariably includes a stop by the great gorge (think *National Lampoon's Vacation*). Even if we've never seen it for ourselves, we've seen enough movies, postcards, textbook photos, and television specials that we have a pretty good idea of what it looks like.

As a result, all of us after López come anticipating "the authentic Grand Canyon experience" as it is defined by the experts—the filmmakers, photographers, and authors. The way we rate our encounter is based, in large part, on how well it conforms to the expectations these experts create. Walker Percy put it something like this:

If it looks just like the postcard, the sightseer is pleased. He feels he has not been cheated. But if it does not conform, he will not be able to see it directly; he will only be conscious of the disparity between what it is and what it is "supposed to be."

What is true of the Grand Canyon, strangely enough, is also true of churches. Many ministers and churchgoers have surrendered their judgment about what constitutes "the authentic church experience" to a small group of experts. These experts write books, speak at conferences, and typically lead large and influential congregations. Because of their success, we imagine them to be great Christian pioneers who are part of something we have never seen—the "real" church experience. Over time, the experts have done for church what postcards and PBS specials have done for the Grand Canyon: They've made it difficult for us to appreciate our own experience because it doesn't measure up to theirs. We have lost the ability to see and judge our success for ourselves. All we can see is the disparity between what our churches *are* and what they are "supposed" to be.

Ambitions and Revisions

I began my ministry career at the tender age of twenty (it seemed like a good idea at the time). When I accepted my first post as pastor, I was entirely seduced by the experts' description of ministry success. No doubt you've heard the story before. There are endless variations in the particulars, but the arc goes something like this: At some point in your life you sense a clear call from God to enter the ministry. It makes a better story if this happens after years of success in a lucrative secular career or a period of profound and sinful rebellion. After a time of preparation—whether in seminary or through a careful perusal of church planting materials—you take a position in a small church. Over the next several years, your ministry grows. You see people reconcile with God, lives are changed, and you feel confident you are squarely within God's will. You've found your calling. Either your church plant grows rapidly or you move from church to church—usually (and fortunately) to increasingly larger, more vibrant congregations. Soon your peers recognize your success and a publisher asks you to write a book about your story. You share it at conferences. You have arrived.

I didn't have the dramatic conversion story, but I was confident in my heart of hearts that this story would someday be mine. I came by the fantasy honestly. After all, I grew up in a congregation that exemplified it. It was small when we joined, but by the time I left for college, our youth group was larger than most churches.

So when I took my first pastorate in a small church in the middle of nowhere, I had a big vision for that rural congregation of fifteen or so. I assumed it needed to grow exponentially, as my home church had. And I assumed it needed everything that made that happen at my home church—midweek programs, professional musicians, a dynamic youth ministry. Never mind that the church didn't have enough members to run a single program, any money, or any youth. I was the expert, after all (or I'd read the experts' books, at least). It was fortunate for them I came when I did. I was God's man, I thought, to lead Anchor Baptist Church to the "real" church experience.

But something happened to me there that I hadn't expected. First, the congregation helped me recognize that the small church is fully equipped to carry out the mission of God in the world. They didn't need me to put them on course. They didn't need to be more staffed or better resourced in order to effectively disciple their current members and make a significant impact on the surrounding community. Everything the church needed had been given it by God. I began to recognize potential and strengths where the experts had trained me to see limitations and liabilities. In fact, I began to believe that the smaller church actually is uniquely equipped to meet the particular ministry challenges of the twenty-first century.

Meanwhile, the Holy Spirit began to impress upon me the profound significance of another story, another way to tell the narrative of God's work in the world. If you're like me, this story probably sounds a little more like your own.

Again, the details vary, but the arc is essentially the same: You feel the same sense of calling and take the time to make the same preparations. After listening to the experts—reading their books and attending their conferences—you apply the principles they identify as the keys to their success. In your ministry, too, lives are changed; people are reconciled to God. Yet success seems always just beyond your reach. No matter what you do, your ministry doesn't grow. And no one validates your faithfulness with their attention. No one ever asks you to speak about how you grew your congregation from 75 to 120 in just seventeen years. As a result, you live with a sense of disappointment. You may doubt your calling and wonder whether you've ranged outside of God's will, because you know well the story the experts have written and have been unable to make it your own.

The overwhelming majority of pastors are living this second story, the narrative of obscurity. According to the Hartford Institute for Religion Research, there are 177,000 churches in America with fewer than 100 weekly worshipers and another 105,000 churches that see between 100 and 500 in attendance each week. On the other hand, there are only 19,000 churches—or 6 percent of the total—with more than 500 attendees. That means that if there were 100 churches in your town, 94 of them would have 500 or fewer attendees, and only six would have more than 500. Mega-churches (regular attendance over 2,000) make up less than one half of one percent of churches in America. The narrative of success may be the one people write books about, but it is not the typical one. We have allowed the ministry experience of 6 percent of pastors to become the standard by which the remaining 94 percent of us judge ourselves.

In my role as an editor for *Leadership* journal, I've talked with pastors from across the denominational spectrum.

Everywhere I go, I hear pastors beginning to question the experts. Though their stories are not often told, I have seen small churches from Chicago to Los Angeles making an enormous impact for the kingdom of God, precisely because they have rejected the advice of the experts. They, too, have begun to see potential where the experts have trained them to see liabilities. Even some large-church pastors are abandoning the predominant metrics of success for new ways of thinking about the work of the church. We'll hear many of these stories in the ensuing pages of this book.

But first we need to deconstruct some of the prevailing assumptions about church ministry success.

Bigger, Better, and the Kingdom of God

While I was writing this chapter, I attended a large pastor's conference on the West Coast. For two days, I worshiped with over 3,000 other men and women who are deeply committed to Christ's work through the local church. At its best, this sort of gathering is sublime. There is something deeply moving about the experience of joining in one voice with a massive crowd of fellow worshipers. The combined energy is empowering and infectious. Theologically, such an experience in a Christian context serves as a foretaste of eternity, when all of earth and heaven will join in the praises of God.

This experience reminded me of what draws us irresistibly to large-church ministry. We love being part of something larger than ourselves. We all want our ministries to matter. When Christ returns, each of us wants to hear him say, "Well done, good and faithful servant." The father of modern missions, William Carey, articulated the desire of every Christian's heart when he challenged his peers to "expect great things *from* God; attempt great things *for* God." And earthly creatures that we are, the surest evidence we have of the significance of our ministries is numeric growth. When our numbers swell, we feel confident that we have invested our talents wisely. When they shrink, we are inclined to believe we need to redouble our efforts. Ultimately, our desire for the measurable results of success is motivated by faithfulness to God's mission and our calling.

But there is a danger in our desire to do big things for God, for our pursuit of success dovetails with a powerful American temptation: the appeal of celebrity. These days, obscurity is the worst kind of failure. When we do something significant, we expect to be rewarded with popularity. It would be easy to blame Hollywood or YouTube for this. But the instinct is as old as America itself. And more to the point, the nation's first celebrity was a preacher. As early as the 1700s, evangelist George Whitefield was already keeping careful (if inflated) count of the crowds that flocked to hear his preaching. The larger the crowds, the more successful he deemed the effort. Whitefield's popularity has left an indelible mark on our self-awareness as pastors.

More recently, Henri Nouwen has said it this way: "Stardom and individual heroism, which are such obvious aspects of our society, are not at all alien to the church. There too the dominant image is that of the self-made man or woman who can do it all alone."[1] What this means is that we want our ministries to matter, sure. But we also want ourselves to matter. By current standards, celebrity is a sure sign of success. And everyone knows that celebrity is hard to come by when the small church is your platform.

The real danger of the appeal of success, though, is that we are tempted to superimpose our own expectations onto the Scriptures. When this happens, we tell the story of the New Testament church as if it followed that familiar path from obscurity to success. When we do this, we assume the Bible affirms our preoccupation with size.

A popular large-church pastor recently said at a conference: "If numbers are not important, then why does the word *numbers* come up so often in Scripture?"[2] On the surface, that seems like a fair question. After all, there appears to be a link in Scripture, particularly in the book of Acts, between the faithfulness of the church and its growth in size. Consider these passages: "And the Lord added to their number daily those who were being saved" (Acts 2:47). "Then the church throughout Judea, Galilee and Samaria enjoyed a time of peace. It was strengthened; and encouraged by the Holy Spirit, it grew in numbers" (Acts 9:31). "So the churches were strengthened in the faith and grew daily in numbers" (Acts 16:5). These passages appear to establish a clear pattern. When the church is faithful, the Spirit works and the church grows.

The Scriptures say, "About three thousand were added to their number that day" when Peter preached at Pentecost (Acts 2:41). Reading backward, it's easy to imagine that what began that day was the first mega-church—Jerusalem Community Fellowship. If we take a closer look at the first chapters of Acts, however, we find that it wasn't a large, central congregation that was born.

The three thousand who became believers after Peter's sermon were from all over the known world and were in Jerusalem for the Jewish festival of Pentecost. Luke tells us that in the crowd that gathered that day there were "Parthians,

Medes and Elamites; residents of Mesopotamia, Judea and Cappadocia, Pontus and Asia, Phrygia and Pamphylia, Egypt and the parts of Libya near Cyrene; [and] visitors from Rome" (Acts 2:9–10). These new believers may have met together for a season, but most of them likely returned home when the festival ended, taking the gospel with them all around the Mediterranean.

Moreover, whatever Christians remained in Jerusalem after Pentecost were dispersed by persecution shortly thereafter. Acts 8:1 says that all the believers except for the apostles "were scattered throughout Judea and Samaria."

These insights should adjust our mental image of the size and success of the early church. The three thousand that responded to Peter's message were dispersed over an area twice the size of Texas and separated by the Mediterranean Sea. Pentecost may have been the first mass revival in history, but it did not create the first mega-church. Instead, Acts 2 records the birth of many small—even micro—congregations. The rest of Acts repeats this theme. Acts 9 tells us that it was not a single church that grew in numbers, but "the church throughout Judea, Galilee, and Samaria." These small congregations didn't meet in a single building. They met in homes, synagogues, and public spaces. In the passages where Scripture records the increase of numbers, it is usually testifying to the growth of the church universal, not a single congregation.

All sincere pastors and church leaders want to see the body of Christ expand. After all, Jesus' final commandment on earth was a call to spread his gospel to our neighbors and to the ends of the earth. But we have to realize that we can be faithful to Christ's Great Commission without centralizing worship to the point that every disciple within a two-hour radius is meeting in the same coliseum-sized building every week.

The apostolic church, those scattered, small, and fervent congregations, spread Christianity throughout the Roman Empire in a matter of a few centuries. Sociologist Rodney Stark estimates that at the end of the first century there may have been only twenty-five thousand Christians in the entire known world. By the fourth century, before the Roman Emperor Constantine legalized the practice of Christianity, there may have been as many as 20 million. This growth occurred through the combined efforts of small churches scattered abroad.

The congregations that made up the early church didn't have the impressive presence many ministries have today through television, radio, and the Internet. They didn't have campuses and facilities and programs. They didn't have educated clergy. God used the combined faithfulness and strength of dozens of under-resourced, poorly staffed, badly programmed, and unprofessional small churches to change the world forever. All they had was the gospel of Christ and the Holy Spirit. That was plenty to expand the kingdom of God across the entire known world. That is plenty still today.

In fact, instead of illustrating the dominant narrative of success, the Bible testifies to the narrative most pastors experience—the narrative of obscurity. Sometimes faithfulness to God's work results in the sudden shrinking of a group of followers. People left Jesus in droves when his teaching struck too near the bone. In John 6, just after Jesus feeds the five thousand and walks on water, he tells his disciples, "I tell you the truth, unless you eat the flesh of the Son of Man and drink his blood, you have no life in you." Nobody had any idea what he was talking about; they were confused and offended. "This is very hard to understand. How can anyone accept it?" (v. 60 NLT). Jesus' hard words had devastating consequences for his ministry: "From this time many of his disciples turned back and no longer followed him" (v. 66).

From our perspective post-Easter, it can be difficult to remember that Jesus' ministry, by all worldly standards, was a profound and extraordinary failure. As he drew his final breaths, he was utterly alone. At one time, he had an impressive following. Everyone knew his name. He attracted crowds wherever he went. But the nearer he drew to the conclusion of his calling, the deeper he slipped into obscurity.

What may be worse for us is that Jesus promises a similar fate for his disciples—and that includes you and me. "All men will hate you because of me," he says in Matthew 10:22. And in Matthew 24:9, "You will be handed over to be persecuted and put to death, and you will be hated by all nations because of me." That message does not sell many books.

I don't mean to be overly dramatic. My point is simply this: Our dominant narrative of success is not supported by the story of the New Testament church. Scripture makes it hard to claim congregation size as a foolproof mark of faithfulness. No doubt all of us can think of large churches that we suspect are large because they have compromised the gospel to draw a crowd. Conversely, we can think of other churches that have grown exponentially precisely because of their faithful preaching of the gospel. And for every small church that fails to grow despite its commitment to outreach and disciple making, there is another that continues to shrink because it is petty, mean, and uninterested in the mission of God. Until we stop measuring our success in terms of numerical size and growth, we may be unable to accurately analyze the faithfulness of our ministry. To paraphrase 1 Corinthians 3:7, the church leader's job is to plant and water, but the increase of the crop is up to God.

New Sight for Sore Eyes

What is at stake here is not simply an academic definition of ministry success or failure. At its core, how we imagine success in the church directly reflects our assumptions about the gospel of Jesus Christ.

After all, an important part of following Jesus is learning to see the truth of things behind appearances. In Christ, the foolish things of the world confound the wise; in Christ, the powerless supplant the powerful; in Christ, the eternal purposes of God are fulfilled in the death of the Messiah. If our ministries are to reflect the values of Jesus, we should be skeptical when we are more "successful" than Jesus was.

Of all Jesus' parables, the one that may be most valuable for disciplining our understanding of ministry success is the story of the mustard seed.

"The kingdom of heaven is like a mustard seed," Jesus explains, "which a man took and planted in his field. Though it is the smallest of all your seeds, yet when it grows, it is the largest of garden plants and becomes a tree, so that the birds of the air come and perch in its branches" (Matthew 13:31–32). The obscure, the small, the insufficient—such are the means God uses to bring about his kingdom. These are words of life for the small church pastor and any other Christian longing to see the results of his or her obedience. Though at first and on the surface the work of God appears insignificant and inconsequential, it mysteriously yields a harvest of overabundance.

In fact, it appears that what God delights in most are the tiny efforts that yield results that only he can take the credit for. Christ's starting lineup was a band of fearful, unqualified disciples. Today, with all of creation at his disposal, he chooses to mediate his message of good news through a community he calls the church. That church—your church and my church, such as it is—is God's mustard seed.

Please do not misunderstand me: I don't mean to say that God is not delighted by large churches or that their ministries are somehow less faithful than those of smaller churches. But in larger churches, ministry success is easier to see because it shows up in ways we know how to measure. I only mean that the parable of the mustard seed should convince us that we can be part of a mighty work of God even when the results of our labor are not readily measurable and impressive. God is not limited by our resources or qualifications.

Embracing the Vision

When we forget the principle of the mustard seed, we risk forcing our own vision of the church, or the prescribed vision of experts, onto our congregation. In our efforts to live the narrative of success, we view the small church not as God's mustard seed but as an obstacle to be overcome. We then rely on our vision to bring about the success we desire. We do this at our peril.

Disturbed over the gap between the church in Acts and the German church in the late 1930s, Dietrich Bonhoeffer wrote *Life Together* to explain genuine Christian community.

In the first section of the book, the person who comes under the fiercest attack is the pastor Bonhoeffer calls the visionary, the person who has "a very definite idea of what Christian life together should be and [tries] to realize it." Bonhoeffer has strong words for this visionary, for the person we might call the "expert" in Christian community:

> The man who fashions a visionary ideal of community demands that it be realized by God, by others, and by himself. He enters the community of Christians with his demands, sets up his own law, and judges the brethren and God Himself accordingly. He acts as if he is the creator of the Christian community, as if his dream binds men together. When things do not go his way, he calls the effort a failure. . . . So he becomes first an accuser of his brethren, then an accuser of God, and finally the despairing accuser of himself.[3]

This visionary could be the pastor or member of a church of any size. The defensive and testy small-church pastor who wants to see his mini congregation become mega is every bit as much the visionary a large-church pastor might be. Similarly, the desire to stay small is just as dangerous as the ambition to grow large. "Every human wish or dream," Bonhoeffer says, "that is injected into the Christian community is a hindrance to genuine community and must be banished if genuine community is to survive."[4]

With Bonhoeffer's words ringing in our ears, our challenge is to learn to see the church as it is. The rest of this book will explore the inherent strengths and strategic value of the smaller church. Perhaps, surprisingly, it is not only small-church pastors who have begun to recognize these strengths.

Some large-church pastors are beginning to realize that small churches are actually better equipped than their larger counterparts for meeting today's ministry challenges. So, as many small churches are straining to become large, a few megachurches are learning to channel the small-church vibe.

It's ironic, if you think about it. Larger churches are spending their considerable financial and personnel resources to re-create the small-church experience. Meanwhile, smaller churches are expending extraordinary energy and resources, burning through clergy and volunteers alike, in an effort to get big. We mustn't let our preoccupation with size cloud the perception of reality that these larger churches are awakening to: The small church is a strategic organism with unique gifts for carrying out God's mission on earth. Instead of trying to imitate large-church ministry, small churches would do well to recognize and capitalize on their own inherent and strategic strengths.

By *strategic,* I don't mean that the exponential numeric growth of an individual congregation is the goal. I simply mean that the small church is uniquely equipped to fulfill the Great Commission. It was grassroots, small-congregation ministries that brought Methodists and Baptists from relative obscurity in the early 1800s to dominance as America's largest denominations by the end of the same century. Today, it is small communities, typically of Pentecostal Christians, that are spreading the gospel like wildfire through the global South. This book assumes that a given local church is committed, as these movements were and are, to making disciples of its current members and to be actively involved in the mission of outreach and evangelism in its community. I hope the examples in this book will help pastors and members of small churches recognize that to participate in great things for the kingdom they do not need great resources, impressive budgets, and expansive campuses and facilities. All the necessary ingredients are in your church right now—for the congregation that has eyes to see.

Of course, there is a challenge inherent in this claim. Embracing small-church ministry may mean facing criticism from colleagues or family members who wish you would move on to a more "successful" ministry. It is difficult to remain content about your mustard seed when birds are landing in another church's branches. Neither am I suggesting that every small church is healthy and effective simply because it's small. It may take real work to capitalize on the strengths of your small church. But the important first step is to recognize that being small is not a liability—it can be a strategic advantage.

Walker Percy used his illustration about the Grand Canyon to describe the role of the educator. The teacher's job is to help people see for themselves—to take the experts' input with a grain of salt and really engage the world afresh. Again, his insights prove helpful for us. The single greatest problem with small churches is perception. Low attendance, small budgets, and limited staff are not, in and of themselves, problematic. What is problematic are the insecurities and defensiveness that result when we fail to live up to expectations of success established by a handful of churches.

As a dear friend and mentor of mine likes to say, you can do two things with expectations. You can meet them, or you can change them. I say we change them. To do that, pastors of smaller churches must help their people learn to see for themselves. Or more precisely, to see the world as Jesus sees it. And that means the pastor must help his people value the mustard seed and view the church as if they were the first people ever to lay eyes on it, to put aside unreasonable expectations, cast their seeds, and trust God for the harvest.

Questions for Reflection for Pastors or Leadership Teams

1. Do you consider yourself and your ministry successful? Why or why not?

2. How do you measure ministry success in your current context? Where do you get the criteria by which you measure success?

3. How closely related are your self-worth and your ministry success? If your church were to stay small forever, how would you feel about yourself as a pastor/leader and as a person?

Chapter Two

Downward Mobility:
Four Ministries Shrink
for the Kingdom's Sake

Despite the fact that the Bible compares the spread of the gospel to the mustard seed, which appears insignificant and unproductive, the dominant expectation of most pastors is that success is measured in terms of numerical growth. Fifty years from now, this may not be the case. We may all look back on our preoccupation with church size in the late twentieth century and say (as we do now about big hair and head-to-toe denim), "What were we thinking?" When the history books are written about our mega ministry efforts in the future, I suspect that the era between the 1970s and the present will appear the anomaly. In the decades preceding the church-growth movement, small-church ministry will prove to have been the norm by necessity. In the decades to come, small-church ministry will be the norm by choice.

There's substance to support this bit of bravado. To begin with, trends in Christian publication suggest that a growing number of men and women in ministry have wearied of the unreasonable burden of perpetual numerical growth. More and more authors are recognizing, as we discussed in the previous chapter, that the Bible's standards for ministry success differ significantly from the dominant expectations of our day. Issues such as leadership development, discipleship, and spiritual formation are moving from the periphery of church priorities toward the center. As that happens, the expectation of extraordinary size is being squeezed out.

But a change in theological convictions may not be the only thing that is altering the future of Christian ministry in America. American Christianity from its beginnings has been as concerned with pragmatism as it has with theological precision. We may not always ask, "Is it biblical?" But we do always ask, "Does it work?" And the fact of the matter is that many people are finding that large-church ministry simply isn't working anymore. For purely practical reasons, smaller is increasingly better.

The goal when talking about any ministry strategy is, of course, to be able to answer yes to these questions: "Is it biblical?" and "Does it work?" What follows are four stories of pastors and ministries that finally recognized the limitations of large-scale ministry and have opted, both for practical reasons and for the kingdom's sake, to leverage the strengths of strategically small ministry.

SINGING A NEW SONG

On nearly every conceivable level, the account of Dave Gibbons' ministry adventures is a typical—almost stereotypical—success story, the kind they write books about.

Before he entered full-time ministry, Dave was making a name for himself as a venture capitalist. "Businessman" was Dave's core identity. "I loved to think about ways to generate capital," he reflects. Better yet, he was good at it. In those days, it seemed that Dave had found his calling.

But a traumatic experience made him reconsider God's plan for his life. Dave's mother, his closest friend, was killed in an automobile accident. The event reoriented the young businessman's priorities. At his mother's funeral, Dave sensed God telling him that the pursuit of wealth had become an idol. Instead of pursuing capital, Dave should be pursuing lost souls. In particular, God put in Dave's heart a passion for people on the margins, people like his mom, who never quite found her place in the traditional church.

Shortly thereafter, Dave left the business world and decided to plant a church. In July 1994, after much prayer and preparation, Dave headed to Irvine, California, with a ten-year plan. His general calling to reach the margins had taken a particular shape. The Los Angeles race riots were still a fresh wound, and Dave desired to bind them by planting and growing a vibrant multiethnic church amid the racial tension.

Dave met his ten-year goal. From a handful of faithful friends who met in the Gibbons' basement, the church ballooned to four thousand members that met on four campuses. In just about a decade, they grew from micro to mega.

The growth was exciting, but it meant that NewSong had to expand. As the church searched for real estate in the competitive Southern California market and pushed to raise $20 million for a building project, Dave became dissatisfied with the path the church was taking. *Is this all my life's going to be?* he wondered. *Am I just trying to build a bigger box where 90 percent of the people still aren't going to be doing anything?*[1]

While he wrestled with his growing uneasiness about the church's future, Dave took a yearlong hiatus to minister in Bangkok, Thailand, where he discovered a new normal. The denomination he was working with was made up of about 4,000 members, roughly the same number as his own four-site church in the United States. But those 4,000 Christians were distributed among nearly 400 churches. Dave felt God speak into his dissatisfaction with NewSong's direction in the form of a question: "Who's stronger—four thousand people in four locations or four thousand people in four hundred different churches?" His time in Thailand convinced him that the answer was clear: Smaller is better.

Dave returned to the U.S. with a new vision that dramatically changed NewSong's ministry trajectory. At the core of Dave's change of heart was a radical realization: For his calling to reach people on the margins, size was a liability. So now instead of continuing to grow NewSong into an ever-larger mega-church, the congregation expands its ministry reach by planting small churches worldwide. NewSong calls these congregations of between 30 and 300 people "verges," because they are "a convergence of the best features of a small and a large church." They provide the critical mass necessary to remain energetic about mission, but they are intimate enough to be conducive to authentic community.

NewSong anticipated a benefit of smaller-scale ministry that became clear to many churches during the economic recession of early 2009: Smaller churches are more resource efficient. This isn't necessarily true in terms of percentages; regardless of size, for example, nearly 70 percent of a congregation's income is committed to overhead, such as staff, facility, and utilities expenses. The difference is a matter of scale. Dave estimates that NewSong was at one time spending nearly $70,000 a month just to keep the church building open. That figure is nearly equivalent to the annual budget of the average church.

But the verges are better stewards. They allow "the accountability and ministry opportunities of small groups," Dave explains, but "eliminate the logistical issues and prohibitive overhead of large groups." This is especially good news when you're trying to reach the fringes. The down-and-out are often economically unable to afford to pay pastor salaries and the overhead that large facilities require.

For Dave, smaller, nimbler congregations are the only way to reach the margins. In fact, he believes that congregations of 300 and smaller are "going to be the most effective in many places around the world. I don't think bigness is going to fit most people or most cultural contexts where the church needs to grow."

PRIESTHOOD OF OUTCASTS

Alan Hirsch found his way into small-church ministry by a very different path.

While he was in seminary, Alan participated in an unconventional ministry with people on the fringes of society in Melbourne, Australia. There Alan experienced firsthand a community that was formed by and committed to Paul's teaching on spiritual gifting in Ephesians 4:11–13:

> It was he who gave some to be apostles, some to be prophets, some to be evangelists, and some to be pastors and teachers, to prepare God's people for works of service, so that the body of Christ may be built up until we all reach unity in the faith and in the knowledge of the Son of God and become mature, attaining to the whole measure of the fullness of Christ.

One of the early founders of that community, a former drug dealer named George, possessed what Alan considered an apostolic gifting. Immediately after George accepted Christ, he started evangelizing his drug-dealing and prostituting friends, and many of them became followers of Christ. Watching George and the other members of that community grow and build up others by exercising their gifts instilled in Alan a hunger to lead a church that was marked by congregational participation and built around people's individual spiritual gifting.

A few years later, Alan accepted the call to pastor South Melbourne Church of Christ. The church made it clear that Alan was their last hope for survival. They were an aging congregation in a changing neighborhood, and they were in a pattern of inevitable decline. So South Melbourne gave Alan simple orders: Either save the church or kill it.

The newly minted seminary graduate was at a loss for direction in his early days at South Melbourne. His education had equipped him with a tool belt of strategies that were intended to yield success through the development and maintenance of organizational systems. But it was fairly clear to Alan that none of those resources was going to do him much good where he was. The church building was in an inner-city neighborhood made up of "yuppies, older working-class folk, subcultural groups, a large gay population, and upper-class snobs."[2] It seemed unlikely that church-growth strategies would reach any of these groups. It seemed even less likely that any one method would reach all of them.

To further complicate things, when he took the pastorate at South Melbourne, the colorful bunch that he worshiped with through seminary joined him there, making the congregation one part aging and committed "church people" and one part young and marginalized new converts. This was not a recipe for success. The question became, "How do we lead and grow such a blessedly diverse group of believers?"

Alan and the leadership team made a couple of creative and courageous efforts to grow the congregation and reach their neighbors early on. All of them were born of the church-growth mentality Alan had been trained in. All of them were top-down endeavors that required significant resources and oversight from the church staff. They didn't encourage the congregational participation Alan hoped for. And ultimately they didn't work.

The church's leadership felt deeply that they were missing their calling. Sure, they had reached people that other churches had not. But in the end, Alan sensed that South Melbourne had become "little more than a worship club for trendy people alienated from the broader expressions of church." Instead of being a congregation marked by active participation, most of the members remained overwhelmingly passive.

In the end, the church's leadership team recognized that their effort to grow the church numerically in a single location was the primary obstacle keeping them from truly embracing mission and participation. So they decided to restructure as a movement of many small congregations. This would allow them to focus on mission, because they would no longer be geographically static. Now the church's members would be distributed throughout the city and could reach their neighbors with greater flexibility.

More churches meant that more leaders were needed. For Alan, this emphasized the importance of organizing each of these small churches around the gifts of their congregants. Decentralizing into small congregations also forced South Melbourne to take leadership development seriously and ultimately engage a greater percentage of the population in the mission of the church. The result has been success of a new stripe altogether, marked by a growing number of small gatherings that reach distinct tribes of people throughout the city.

South Melbourne Church of Christ is not the only congregation to recognize the limitations of large-church ministry for spiritual formation and leadership development. The primary avenue for member participation in larger churches is through programs and church activities. The expectation in these environments is that programs and activities will lead to spiritual growth, which will result in members taking ownership of the church's mission. Unfortunately, this strategy doesn't necessarily work.

The Willow Creek Association's 2007 *REVEAL* Study was based on more than 11,000 congregations that completed surveys targeted to identify the typical pattern of spiritual development in churches. In the end, the WCA determined what Alan Hirsch suspected all along: "Involvement in church activities does not predict or drive long-term spiritual growth."[3]

This reality is one of the primary motivations behind the growing missional movement, of which Alan is a notable spokesperson. These communities are driven by the twin commitments of the priesthood of all believers and the primacy of the mission of the church. They feel the church has fallen short of its calling by relegating all its ministry and mission to a couple of professional Christians. To correct this trend, they want to see all people equipped and released to embrace their role in the royal priesthood.

KEEPING IT SIMPLE

Neil Cole became a Christian during college and grew in his faith at a vibrant mega-church near campus. After college he attended seminary to prepare for the ministry and suspected that someday he would be working in a large-church environment. What he didn't imagine is that he would eventually end up on staff at the mega-church he attended in college.

Early in his ministry, it became clear that Neil had a special gift and passion for evangelism. Leaders in Neil's denomination recognized this gift, so they asked him to oversee church planting in Southern California and Arizona. Neil was thrilled. He used every tool his training and experience had provided him to make his first effort a success.

Success depended on providing an impressive worship experience and putting the right factors in place from the beginning to accommodate inevitable growth. "We really wanted our first plant to succeed," Neil recalled in an interview with *Leadership* journal, "so we poured in a lot of money. We paid for two full-time pastors, a sound system, worship teams, lots of publicity, consultants, and toolkits." Unfortunately, despite the careful planning and Neil's best efforts, the church never took root. Just one year later, it died.

This experience was a turning point for Neil. "I think God wanted to teach us something," Neil says. "We learned a church cannot be bought; it must be planted. And that means starting small." With that, Neil abandoned the bigger-is-better mentality and launched a ministry that has made his vision for church planting a reality. The big shift for Neil was a change of understanding regarding what is essential to a church plant. One key ingredient is size—small size.

Neil's organization, Church Multiplication Associates (CMA), oversees and encourages the planting of small, simple churches. The churches, which Neil calls "organic," don't require buildings; they meet in homes, coffeehouses, and rented spaces. And because they don't require buildings, they can be planted and maintained with limited resources.

Not only are the churches small and inexpensive; they are also simple. The trouble with the average church, in Neil's mind, is that it requires a trained professional to run. But CMA's churches are kept simple enough that anyone with pastoral gifting can lead them. And for this reason, perhaps, many of the churches remain small. But Neil is fine with that. "The church is meant to grow," he writes in *Organic Church*. But he adds, "This doesn't mean that every local church should keep getting bigger and bigger."[4] As Neil sees it, evangelism doesn't lead to bigger churches. It leads to more churches.

Small, simple churches are the most effective means Neil can imagine for fulfilling his primary mission: evangelism. Neil and CMA are bent on filling the earth with God's kingdom. And for that, as Neil sees it, the smaller the churches, the better. "Because it is not financially encumbered with overhead costs and is easily planted in a variety of settings, [the organic church] reproduces faster and spreads further."

Viral reproduction—not accumulation—will take the gospel to the ends of the earth.

INTIMACY IS THE NEW EXCELLENCE

By the mid-1990s, Willow Creek Community Church in South Barrington, Illinois, had run up against a challenge that had stymied most churches at the time: how to reach the ever-elusive Generation X. Willow Creek was the flagship church-growth success story. But even so, the church wasn't seeing twenty- and thirty-somethings in its corporate worship, and they worried, like most congregations do, about the church's future if it failed to attract the next generation.

In 1996, the church launched what it hoped would be the answer to the Gen-X conundrum. The Saturday night worship service was called Axis, and it was characteristically Willow Creek insofar as it was based on the assumption that if you provide a worship experience that your target audience finds appealing and engaging, they will come in droves. What made it different was the tone of the service. Listen to how *WILLOW* magazine described the Axis worship experience in 2001:

> As the band starts to take its place on the stage, an air of anticipation flows through the crowd, quickly augmented by fast, rough-edged, recorded music interrupted only by video footage featuring "postmoderns" voicing their disillusionment with life and skepticism regarding the church's ability to change them or their circumstances. The band follows with an equally hard-edged instrumental, then an energy-generating song in which the singer cries out for a response to God's love.[5]

The end goal of Axis was to provide a place where twenty-somethings felt safe to worship, so that when they aged and started families, they would transition into the congregational life of Willow Creek proper. The ministry was only partially effective.

At its high point in 2001, nearly 2,000 young people gathered for worship at Axis every Saturday night. But church leaders soon recognized that as the Axis crowd aged, they were not moving into the regular Willow services. In fact, it seems they were simply disappearing. By 2006, attendance had diminished to around 400. That same year, the church pronounced the ministry dead in its original form.

John Peacock, Axis's one remaining staff member, reimagined the ministry from the ground up. Instead of focusing all its attention on a single corporate worship experience, he believed the solution was to go small. Axis became a ministry distributed. Now attending young people meet in twenty-five small group locations—what they call missional community hubs—throughout the Chicago suburbs. Once a month, the hubs meet together for a worship time called the Axis Experience, but even this corporate meeting has been scaled down.

In retrospect, organizers of the first Axis effort recognize that they understood their target demographic to an extent. They understood that Gen-Xers value honesty and raw emotion in their worship experiences. But what they understand now is that, in the end, this generation doesn't value worship experiences in general nearly as much as they crave genuine relationships. When it came to meeting that relational need, the ministry's size was an obstacle.

"We've learned to break these things down into smaller

communities where people actually know each other," Peacock explains.[6] "Many people in this generation are already coming in with distrust toward God and the church. The more relational environments we have, the more trust can be built and people will be more open to exploring Christianity."

Axis organizers have realized that size is not only a liability when it comes to facilitating relationships. It can also stand in the way of making disciples. Peacock explains that one of the biggest mistakes contemporary churches make is in their leadership and organizational structure. "You have a business-run, top-down, bottom-line culture, yet you're trying to bring around a loving, transformative culture in your community. It just doesn't work." To reach young people, the church's behavior in all areas must harmonize with and reinforce its stated values.

The failure of the first iteration of Axis is one example of an increasingly familiar pattern. In parts of the South and West (including Colorado, Southern California, and Texas), the regions of the country with the highest concentrations of mega-churches, the home church movement is growing. What's more, the unlikely and ironic source of home-church growth appears to be the mega-churches themselves.

In her 2006 *Time* article, "Why Home Churches Are Filling Up," Rita Healy explains that mega-churches are "made possible by hundreds of small 'cell groups' that meet off-nights and provide a humanly scaled framework for scriptural exploration, spiritual mentoring, and emotional support."[7] These groups become the true center of religious life and supplement the "entertaining if sometimes undemanding" impersonal mass gatherings on the weekends. For the most part, these smaller gatherings reinforce and improve the vitality of the mega-church. But in some cases, they have "decided to lose the mother church."

The folks who gather in these home churches recognize that their true needs—for belonging, accountability, and intimacy—can be met in the small group itself. For that reason, they see little use for the large group celebration. For a growing number of people, if forced to choose between impressive, large-group worship gatherings and small, intimate communities, they will choose the intimacy of community every time. The benefits of large-church gatherings are not worth sacrificing the boon of the small community.

WHERE ARE YOU GOING WITH ALL THIS?

Though they arrived at their conclusions from different directions and for different reasons, Dave, Alan, Neil, and the Axis team all learned the same lesson. In order to effectively carry out the ministry they had been called to, the standard expectation of church growth was an obstacle. Together their stories highlight several key advantages of smaller-scale ministry.

In his experience with NewSong, Dave Gibbons recognized that smaller congregations are more nimble and resource efficient, making them the model of choice for ministry on the margins.

Alan Hirsch became convinced that the smaller unit is more conducive to identifying and developing people's spiritual gifting, making a small size advantageous for involving more people in the mission of the church.

Through his efforts with the Church Multiplication Associates, Neil Cole determined that small, simple churches are better positioned for evangelism and church reproduction.

And through the failure of its first efforts at the Axis ministry, Willow Creek learned that smaller, more intimate gatherings are more desirable for reaching Generation X and the generations to follow.

In other words, small churches are uniquely equipped to carry out what are perhaps the three most important functions of the church: evangelism, discipleship (including leadership development), and passing the faith from one generation to the next.

KINGDOM GROWTH

Another thing these ministers and ministries share in common is a growing sense of the distinction between the local church and the kingdom of God. It is easy to confuse the two. When we become busy with our weekly responsibilities and long-term plans, we can easily forget that God is at work even where we are not. But choosing to leverage the strength of small size means acknowledging that the kingdom of God extends far beyond our own church and its efforts. The kingdom must grow. But that doesn't mean that every church will be growing numerically all the time.

On the personal level, where the church leader's heart is concerned, we like to receive credit for our efforts. There is nothing necessarily sinful about wanting our hard work to be noticed. If there is, you won't hear me saying so. I thrive on positive feedback and affirmation. As I said before, we all want God to tell us, "Well done, good and faithful servant." But it sure is nice to hear a "well done" from our friends and colleagues now and then, as well. Unfortunately, when pastors are truly faithful to the kingdom call, looking out for the church universal rather than only their local congregations, the fruit of their labors often goes unnoticed by those around them. But we can always rely on the fact that God "is not unjust; he will not forget your work and the love you have shown him as you have helped his people and continue to help them" (Hebrews 6:10).

Consider this example. This past summer, our church invited a nearby small church of another denomination to participate in our Vacation Bible School. This church sent children and volunteers who learned and served alongside our own folks, and the congregations enjoyed their time together.

On the final afternoon of VBS, the kids performed a short program for the parents who could be there. Our pastor was out of town, but the pastor of the other church, Jeff, was in attendance. Our VBS director (my wife) invited Jeff to offer the closing prayer. Before he did, he thanked everyone for coming and gave them the weekend service times for both churches. As far as our congregations were concerned, we didn't care where these families—most of them without a church home— decided to attend. We would consider it kingdom gain if they came to faith in either church.

THE GRASS IS ALWAYS GREENER

The four stories above are radical examples of ways that churches are opting for small-scale ministry in an effort to make large-scale impact. But even more churches are making modest changes in this direction. According to the Hartford

Institute for Religious Research, mega-churches continue to grow in size and number. But their strategies are changing.

First, instead of building ever-larger facilities, mega-churches are channeling their growing numbers into multiple sites. The most obvious reason for this is that as real estate costs escalate, perpetual growth becomes unrealistic. Thus the secondary locations tend to be considerably smaller and cheaper than the primary location. In some cases, mega-churches are even opting for smaller facilities simply to appeal to people's preferences for more intimate worship spaces. One congregation near Los Angeles, whose attendance numbers more than 10,000 every weekend, recently built a 500-seat chapel to provide a smaller-scale, quieter experience for people who prefer intimacy in worship.

Second, mega-churches are putting more and more energy into small groups. As the *Time* article quoted earlier explained, mega-churches find their vitality in cell groups. Large group worship services are exciting, but they are not conducive to spiritual growth. That, mega-churches are finding, takes place in smaller, more intimate relationships.

With both of these innovations—toward smaller meeting spaces and more emphasis on small groups—mega-churches are capitalizing on just a few of the unique strengths of the small church: financial efficiency, evangelistic energy, and personal intimacy. In other words, while membership rolls may be increasing in mega-churches, these massive organizations have recognized the limits and liabilities of being large; as a result, they are taking steps to emulate the small church in strategic ways. In the remaining chapters of this book, we'll hear the stories of smaller churches that are putting their size—or lack thereof—to work in creative and surprising ways.

Questions for Reflection for Pastors or Leadership Teams

1. Which of the four stories above did you relate to most? Why?

2. Where do evangelism and discipleship happen most effectively in your church? (Don't consider only formal church programs.)

3. How effective is your church in passing the faith from one generation to the next? Where do you see this currently happening best?

Chapter Three

Keeping It Real:
The Authentic Church

Being ten miles from the nearest streetlight was not the church's biggest problem. There was actually something idyllic about the scene the little white building created, situated as it was in an open meadow flanked by rice fields, forest, and flooded marsh. It was quaint and charming.

There was, however, nothing charming about the worship service.

Some mornings there was a proper musician—someone with sufficient training to caress the old and tuneless piano until it made something like music. But many mornings he was working a paying gig elsewhere. On those Sundays, our worship leader was one of two women whose primary qualifications were having a pulse and being willing to choose hymns ten minutes before the service began. Whichever of them arrived at the church first would open the *Heavenly Highways* hymnal (we had other hymnals, but they liked this one best) and select a few numbers for us to sing. Sometimes there was accompaniment; to be honest, it was better when there wasn't. It was no good adding the piano and complicating things with a melody in a fixed key.

Perhaps worse, their song choices were obscure. "Bringing in the Sheaves" was a favorite. I'm still not sure what sheaves are or why we wanted them in.

Oh, and our sound man was a local disc jockey who was short on teeth.

I would show up week after week in my best suit and starched shirt to preach a finely tuned (if mediocre) sermon, and the service would begin with one of the women leading "Bringing in the Sheaves" in two keys at once.

Bear in mind that my vision at this point was still trained on exponential growth. I didn't know how to make that happen, but I was sure of one thing: We weren't going to get there this way. More than once I wanted to stop the music and scream, "Work with me, people!"

They had no musicians and no musicality. I had little stage presence or charisma. This situation may sound familiar. If it does, you know that it's a foolproof recipe for keeping your church small—lousy church music followed by amateur preaching.

Even so, we were something no other church could be. We were ourselves—unashamedly, unapologetically, and unalterably ourselves.

And strangely enough, it worked. The church never experienced extraordinary growth, but it wasn't long before college students rivaled the locals for the largest demographic in the congregation. Youth even began to trickle in. More important, men and women (mostly men) from the community connected with God through the ministry of the members of Anchor Baptist Church.

It may be that twenty years ago our small and haphazard operation would not have appealed to anyone, much less young people. But a new value has emerged that is permeating all of society, from how we determine what products and services we buy, to how we judge and conduct relationships, and even to what we look for in a church. Anchor Baptist Church appealed to this value: authenticity. Small churches in every town are uniquely positioned to be authentic churches.

FROM EXCELLENCE TO AUTHENTICITY

The cultural value of authenticity is complex and far reaching. It has tendrils and blossoms in every arena of contemporary life, making it very difficult to distinguish causes and effects. At the risk of oversimplification, what follows is a brief sketch of the emerging value of authenticity.

Authenticity in the Marketplace

A generation ago, the competitive advantage in business went to the company that could produce the highest quality product for the lowest price. Achieving excellence was the goal for manufacturers and service providers alike, because consumers looked first and foremost for quality and dependability in the products they purchased. They might sacrifice other values, such as fashion (as evidenced by old photos of my parents and even myself) or luxury, but quality was nonnegotiable. They wouldn't be caught dead spending their hard-earned money on things they considered junk.

The desire for excellence is being supplanted by a new consumer value. Authors James Gilmore and Joseph Pine claim, in their bestselling book, *Authenticity*, that instead of searching solely for high-quality goods and services, "people increasingly make purchase decisions based on how real or fake they perceive various offerings."[1] If a generation ago they wouldn't buy junk, today they won't pay for things they consider phony.

The consumer quest for authenticity plays out in several ways. For one, more and more products are advertised as if they arrive in our homes just as nature intended. My wife uses Pure & Natural body wash and EverPure shampoo and conditioner. We drink 100% Pure Florida orange juice and certified organic milk.

Other products emphasize their status as cultural originals or standard-bearers that are "authentically" American—think Coca-Cola ("Can't beat the real thing") and Wrangler ("Real. Comfortable. Jeans.") and Hanes (I'm wearing the "Authentic Tagless T-shirt" as I write).

Related to this is the appeal of all things "vintage." For many, things seem real because they are old. For example, now that we speak of music in terms of mp3 files, there is something appealing about the incarnate, organic hiss of an LP on the record player. Many people will pay more for blue jeans that are old and faded, because they look authentically broken in.

But consumers want more than genuine products. They also want to do business in ways that feel more "real."

According to Gilmore and Pine, the companies that are thriving today find ways to deliver personalized and intimate service to their customers. Instead of the efficient automated telephone services, for example, more consumers want to talk to real people, even if it takes longer. In a technological, digitized world, people long to do business the old-fashioned way: person to person.

Authenticity in Relationships

The consumer's search for authenticity in commerce has its parallel in relationships. Emerging generations long for genuine human connection. But as you might imagine, when it comes to relationships, the concept of authenticity becomes even more complicated. There the term assumes a wide range of related qualities, including transparency, sincerity, vulnerability, and even rawness, messiness, and complexity. In place of superficial compatibility—the "You're okay; I'm okay" mentality that I was raised on—the emerging generation longs for real dialogue, even when the result is confrontation and conflict. Where previous generations valued a certain level of decorum, younger ones want to hear a person's feelings unscripted and unfiltered. They can be impatient and suspicious of cordiality or politeness that seems to hide a person's true feelings.

Such suspicion makes sense when you consider the world many younger people grew up in. We learned from Watergate and Whitewater to distrust our leaders, and from the Rodney King nightmare and the O. J. Simpson trial to limit our confidence in the American justice system. After the shootings at Columbine High School and New Life Church, the bombing of the Alfred P. Murrah building in Oklahoma City, and the terrorist attacks of September 11, 2001, we learned that we aren't safe anywhere.

It's no wonder the emerging generation is suspicious, sarcastic, and unimpressed. Reared amid posturing, pretense, and the hollow promise of unlimited success, they are hungry for relationships that acknowledge the messiness and uncertainty of the human condition.

True Religion: Biblical Authenticity

The emerging culture's hunger for authenticity poses a significant challenge for churches. The message is clear: If what you're offering is phony religion, we aren't interested. Fortunately, appealing to authenticity is not simply another market-savvy strategy to attract the young. Instead, it should remind us of the biblical call to authenticity in our faith. Perhaps nowhere in Scripture is this call clearer than in the book of James.

James doesn't tell us explicitly who his audience is. We only know that he is writing to a handful of congregations that are "scattered abroad." Maybe they fled Jerusalem because of the persecution described in Acts 8. Maybe they are at the fringes of the empire. Whoever and wherever they are, they all have a couple of things in common. For one, they are experiencing hardship of some sort, perhaps even persecution. But what is worse, in James' mind, is that they are failing to practice what they preach.

Though he never uses the word *authenticity*, it's clear that James' concern is similar to ours today. He wants his hearers to live the real, genuine, authentic Christian experience.

His letter is a passionate plea to these believers to wake up to their hypocrisy and become a true community of Christ, one that proves its faith by striking a harmony of belief and action.

In his classic conversation about the relationship between faith and works, James paints a scenario that is all too familiar to us: "Suppose a brother or sister is without clothes and daily food" (2:15). There are two ways a Christian can respond. The first involves speech. More to the point, it *only* involves speech. We simply say, "Go, I wish you well; keep warm and well fed." This is sort of like when someone shares a deep need with us and we say, "Bless your heart. I'll be praying for you." This kind of religion doesn't do anyone any good.

The right way to respond is to meet the physical need. Action is the evidence of true faith. False religion makes empty claims about its beliefs. According to James, true religion doesn't claim or posture or pontificate. It simply acts. True religion puts its money where its mouth is.

True Religion Today

I can't imagine a timelier message for the American church today. At different points in our history, we have been confused about our identity. We have felt pressure from culture to conform and support national goals. We have felt compelled to police the nation's morals, entertain the over-stimulated, and provide therapy for the coddled. In the meantime, the world has begun to see through our efforts to be relevant and respectable, perceiving at some level that we have sold our birthright for a spot at the table. It hears us speaking one message with our tongues and sees us living another with our conduct.

For example, outsiders are well aware that the church claims everyone is welcome. They know that Jesus welcomed sinners with open arms. In *They Like Jesus but Not the Church*, Dan Kimball relates a time when he asked a group of unchurched young people to give their impressions of a few key words. First he asked them about Jesus. The response was overwhelmingly positive. "He is beautiful," they said. And "I want to be like him."

But when he asked them what they thought of Christians, the reflections were unsettling. "They took the teachings of Jesus and turned them into dogmatic rules," one student replied. Another said, "Christians don't apply the message of love that Jesus gave."[2]

Kimball acknowledges that most of these young people had never read the New Testament. Even so, they perceived a marked disparity between what they knew about Jesus and what they found in his disciples. Where Jesus embraced sinners and outcasts, the church has developed a reputation for being suspicious and even fearful of outsiders. If we ever hope for the world to perceive our churches as "real," we must learn to bring our behavior in line with our beliefs.

Because authenticity, like beauty, is to some degree in the eye of the beholder, different people find it in different places. This means that when it comes to churches, no one tradition or congregation will appeal to everyone. Today, some folks are finding authentic Christianity in ancient and liturgical forms of the faith. Many young people are migrating from larger, more casual evangelical churches toward Roman Catholic, Anglican, and Orthodox churches. These worshipers are attracted to the history and rootedness that being part of a centuries-old tradition provides. Connection with the past authenticates these expressions of the faith.

Others are finding genuine fellowship in quite the opposite place—home churches. These worshipers consider the history of Christianity to be a long story of the church's departure from New Testament teaching. They find authentic faith by stripping away the cultural baggage of traditional church and boiling Christian fellowship down to intimate community.

Wherever they find it, though, authenticity is a consistent factor in a person's choice to join a worshiping community. In his book *Lost and Found: The Younger Unchurched and the Churches that Reach Them*, Ed Stetzer writes, "One hundred percent of churches [we] interviewed, deemed effective at reaching young people by our criteria, hold authenticity as one of their highest values or has a commitment to being authentic."[3]

Fortunately for us, if you want your church to be authentic, it's good to be small.

GOOD NEWS FOR SMALL CHURCHES

The pursuit of excellence in business over the last couple decades was fertile soil for the church-growth movement. Churches looked to the business world for guidance in church development, assuming the methods that worked to expand corporations would do the same for churches. They were right. Young professionals in the 1970s and 1980s looked for the same qualities in their churches that they sought in their clothes, automobiles, and home furnishings: excellence. The churches that have grown the largest since then have typically done so by offering an exceptional worship experience. If churches wanted to compete in the marketplace of goods and services, their speakers had to be articulate, their musicians polished, their programs efficient, and their facilities comfortable and inviting.

What was good for large churches was bad for smaller churches. With their limited resources and aging facilities, small churches were unable to compete in the excellence game. They couldn't afford, find, or keep well-trained clergy, professional musicians, or impressive facilities with state-of-the-art sound systems. These churches may have retained their current members, but there were ever fewer new members to replace the aging faithful.

But the authenticity game has leveled the playing field. Simply put, big churches have more obstacles to overcome in order to appear authentic. Many people today will be less enamored of the outward appearances that were so successful at bringing in the crowds ten years ago. People certainly haven't abandoned their demand for excellence altogether, but they are recognizing that "excellence" can be a veneer for phoniness.

The population that is distrustful of authority and was raised hearing upwards of 850 advertising messages a day is skeptical of glam and spin. Many young worshipers are turned off by over-produced worship music and a speaker who is too polished. Smoothness and precision can come across as insincere. Music and light displays that are cued to the second can communicate that performers are less concerned with the congregation's need to experience God than they are with pulling off a masterful performance.

These seekers will excuse unprofessional church music and preaching if they sense the congregation is worshiping from the heart. So former liabilities have become assets. A larger church will have to work even harder to ensure that its authenticity shines through its professionalism. On the other hand, many people will consider a small church's intimacy and ability to respond to the needs of its people as intrinsically genuine. In other words, a small church doesn't have to *become* authentic. It really needs to *stay* authentic. Or to put it the other way around, it needs to stop trying to be something it isn't.

Cultivating Intimacy

Authentic churches are marked by intimacy of fellowship. And because size almost always works against intimacy, small churches are uniquely equipped to cultivate intimate relationships among their congregants.

One way I've seen authentic churches communicate their commitment to intimate fellowship is by inviting members and visitors to share stories of God's grace in their lives. The smaller church environment is particularly conducive to this. My church of around 300 members regularly makes an effort to have a variety of people stand before the congregation to tell us where they've been, what Christ is doing in their lives, and how we can walk with them on their journey.

One particularly powerful season in our church came when the pastor was preaching a series on grace. Each week he emphasized a different aspect of grace, including adoption, forgiveness, and salvation. Before each sermon, a member of the congregation shared a story that illustrated the sermon's theme in his or her own life. On the Sunday dedicated to adoption, an elder statesman in the congregation shared how he was adopted by his sister as a child. Her choosing to take on the burden of loving him unconditionally has been a powerful image of God's love throughout his life as a Christian.

On another Sunday, on the topic of forgiveness, a woman shared how her messy and painful divorce had made it difficult for years to forgive or experience Christ's forgiveness herself. She shared the continuing story of how the Holy Spirit has been empowering her to forgive her ex-husband and how, at the same time, she is becoming ever more aware of God's great forgiveness.

I don't remember the content of many of those sermons, but I'll never forget those stories. They affirmed that each of us comes from somewhere and that we are all on a journey together in and toward the cross. And they made our shared faith personal and immediate; they gave us shared stories and served as a powerful reminder that we are all works in progress. Of course, large churches also use such testimonials in their services. But there's something about the intimacy of the smaller congregation—perhaps the fact that most people actually know the person speaking—that makes these stories more poignant.

Responding to Need

Recalling James, a skeptical population will need more than just to hear our stories. They will also need to see our convictions in action. One advantage small churches enjoy is their ability to respond quickly to community needs. Prompt reply communicates genuine concern because it suggests that helping is instinctive. And while larger churches usually have to mediate outreach through a special program, small congregations can include participation from the entire body.

Every Sunday afternoon for several weeks, I met with three other men from church to pray. The subjects of our prayers were three men in our community who were not a part of our church. We wanted to see them reconnect with God, but we weren't sure what role we should play. So we decided to pray for them for a season, asking God to show us how we could reach out to them in meaningful ways.

At the end of our season of prayer, we received word that one of the men had fallen on hard times. He had prostate cancer. The good news was it could be eradicated with surgery. The bad news was he drove a log truck for a living, and the doctor forbade him to drive in that bouncy cab for nearly two months. The man and his wife depended on his income. There seemed to be no way they could survive if he didn't work.

When the men of the church heard news of this, they called an emergency business meeting, and the dozen or so members who were present that Sunday gathered in the fellowship hall.

"How much can you give?" one of them asked. Everyone dug deep. Even though this man was not a member of our church, he was our neighbor. And that was enough for these folks. Throughout his recovery period, members of the church—not out of the church budget, but from their own pockets—provided groceries, mortgage money, meals, and other tangible support.

Their genuine care and concern was a powerful draw for outsiders. At the end of his recovery, the man joined our fellowship. The two other men we had been praying for, after they saw how the congregation cared for their neighbor, soon became regular attendees themselves and, more important, renewed their commitments to Christ. About that time, a few of the college students who began attending the church to support me told me, "We came here for you; but if you leave, we're staying here." The church's concern for its neighbors, evidenced by their immediate response to need, had made an impression.

The important thing to note is that the care for this trucker was not an isolated incident. On another occasion, the church organized an old-fashioned barn-raising to rebuild a non-member neighbor's house after a flood. Their response was evidence of a culture of care for the parish. There were more impressive churches in the area. But perhaps none so authentic. And that made all the difference.

Whatever You Do, Don't . . .

There are several strategic blunders churches can make as they strive for authenticity. The trouble is these are fairly instinctive efforts, things we'll all be tempted to do. But avoid them at all cost, for they will undermine your efforts to "be real."

The first is this: Don't try to be relevant. Now before you object, what I mean is, don't be trendy. Many churches confuse relevance with trendiness and end up with the latter, because it is far easier to achieve. True relevance is being sensitive to the culture or subculture in which you are ministering and incarnating your ministry in your specific location. It is vital that a church be relevant by that definition, and we'll talk about that more in a later chapter.

Trendiness, by contrast, is applying a strategy that is foreign to your personality and mission for no other reason than to draw a crowd. The worst thing a small church can do is try to reach people by pretending to be like them. A church should welcome everyone; however, they shouldn't *become* everyone. A young person will be open to hearing the gospel from a fifty-year-old pastor who speaks and dresses in a way befitting a fifty-year-old man, if—and this is a big "if"—that pastor and his church show genuine concern for that young person. But that same visitor will smell phoniness from down the street if the middle-aged pastor speaks and dresses like a twenty-year-old in an effort to appear "relevant." Dan Kimball puts it this way in *They Like Jesus but Not the Church*: "It doesn't matter how young and hip you are. What matters is that a person perceives you are genuinely concerned about and interested in him or her."[4]

I was blessed to see this principle confirmed in our congregation in recent months. One Sunday morning, a fellow about my age wandered into the sanctuary early. He wore baggy jeans and a football jersey. He was pierced and tattooed in a lot of places, which is not a big deal. But you must bear in mind that we're Presbyterian with all that implies: liturgical, formal, pressed, starched, and tucked in.

He and I hit it off, and he sat with me through the service. In the course of the morning, I learned that he was a recovering alcoholic, was just getting back on his feet after being homeless for some months, and was in the thick of battle against depression and substance abuse. What's more, he was trained in "the healing arts" and worked with crystals.

He was outside my expertise.

When the service began, he fumbled through our bulletin, dropping and scattering the inserts at the worst of times. He was always a little slow to stand or sit and couldn't find the hymns or the Scripture passage for the sermon. I didn't think things were going well.

After the service, though, the woman seated in front of us (a middle-aged mother of two) turned around and welcomed our visitor. She told him she would love to hear his story sometime; he told her his story was a rough one.

Without missing a beat, she said, "There are a lot of rough stories here." Then she added, "That's what I love about this church. People are very transparent about their pain."

In the narthex during the coffee hour, he met several other church members, including one who suffered from depression just like he did.

As I was walking him out, he said to me, "People didn't have to be so nice to me." He looked down at his clothes. "I'm dressed like this and I don't look like I belong. But I can tell that people here care about me." He added, "There's a sweet spirit here."

Actually, he said, "There's a real positive energy here." But that was close enough for me.

A second big mistake is running a small church like a large church. This is a particular temptation for mid-sized churches on the cusp of moving from small to large. These churches will often divide the congregation into committees and focus groups and develop systems of authority and ministry, so that as the church grows they are prepared for the changing needs of the congregation. They do this in the right spirit, but the result can be unmitigated disaster.

A friend of mine once attended a church plant made up of about thirty regular attendees. The pastor, who was bent on turning his micro community into a mega one, decided it was time to launch a small-group ministry. After all, small groups are a proven ingredient of church growth. So he divided the thirty or so members into seven small groups. The fracturing of the congregation that resulted effectively destroyed their intimacy.

When a pastor fails to recognize the benefits of the small congregation and insists on running it like a large ministry, he will ultimately undermine and obscure the church's strengths. Rather than creating a mega ministry, a think-big strategy can destroy the church's spirit. In this case, the advice our mothers gave us before our first date is apt: "Just be yourself."

The Irony of Authenticity

Telling a person or a congregation to be authentic is a lot like telling them not to think about an aching tooth. The harder they try, the less likely they are to succeed. Or to come at it another way, the pursuit of authenticity is a lot like the pursuit of humility. If you try to become the most humble person in the world, you're doomed to failure before you even begin. This is especially true if you have ulterior motives for becoming humble or, in our case, authentic. If we go to great lengths to make our churches authentic in order to attract people, we'll defeat the purpose. There is nothing more inauthentic than trying to be authentic *for some other reason.*

In other words, authenticity is not a strategy. My point is simply to encourage us to recognize that now is the time to stop pretending, to start thinking critically about the way our congregation's behavior aligns with its stated values, and to become the churches Christ has been urging us to be all along. So, don't pursue authenticity. Pursue Christ. To grossly oversimplify the matter, perhaps our guideposts in this effort are the two greatest commandments: Love God. Love your neighbor. If, as they pursue Christ together, a congregation holds everything they do against these two goals, they will learn where their deeds do and do not match their words.

Loving God comes first. This means each congregation should follow their own convictions when it comes to style of worship, preaching, and church structure. If a congregation isn't comfortable adopting a practice that other, larger churches seem to be doing—singing worship songs, for instance, rather than hymns—then they should probably stick with hymns. If a small church finds out that the key to success for a larger church in town is short, exciting sermons, they shouldn't give up their long and weighty sermons simply to attract new people. The same goes for how Communion is conducted, baptisms are held, and the offering is collected. These are important issues that are a matter of remaining faithful to God and his commands. If we change the way we understand these things, it should be because our convictions about God's revelation have changed and not because current trends are now leading in a new direction.

In the same way, we must find authentic ways to love our neighbors rather than following formulas established outside our communities. To take one example, social justice has become a hot topic in Christian ministry circles recently. And much of this has to do with a growing awareness of the challenges of ministry in urban areas. That means that in a community like Brown Springs, Arkansas, where Anchor Baptist Church meets, caring for neighbors will look very different than it would in Chicago. It's no good running a soup kitchen for the homeless if homelessness isn't an issue in your area. Even so, every community has needs. Loving our neighbors means considering their needs—not adopting the latest trend—before we launch our ministry initiatives.

Eventually, when a church focuses its efforts on loving God in spirit and truth and loving their neighbors as themselves, they become an authentic community almost by accident.

CONCLUSION

Seeking authenticity is a terrible demand. It is far easier to hide behind the glitz and glam of a professional worship service. Performance can mask superficial discipleship and obscure the lack of intimacy in a church. But being committed to being authentic requires real work. Surely, though, such work is more rewarding than trying to keep up with all the latest trends.

To truly exude authenticity, a congregation must bring its actual behavior in line with its stated values. If a church claims on its Web site, in printed materials, or from the pulpit that its passion is connecting people with God, then that commitment must be evident in the church's worship, programs, and community life. It's hard to maintain that we are authentic when we claim to be a family but run our organization as if it were a business. And it's difficult to claim to be authentic when we say we welcome everyone but then market ourselves and shape our services and programs to appeal to specific demographics. These are the things that people will see when they peer deep beneath the surface. If what they find there is fake, they likely won't give us a second chance.

In short, the cultural value of authenticity applies a healthy pressure to the church: the pressure to be faithful to the original mission of God. It is an opportunity to do something many of us have needed to do for a long time—to demote many of the things that have hindered us from genuine service to their rightful place and put our whole energy into the work of the kingdom.

Questions for Reflection for Pastors or Leadership Teams

1. Think about the last few people or families who` have joined your church. What reasons did they give for joining? What do their answers indicate about what your church does well?

2. Are you currently doing anything in your church—whether it's running a program, changing your worship or preaching style, or something else—simply to be fashionable? How has that affected your community life? What would be lost if you stopped doing it?

3. In what areas does your church need to bring its actual behavior in line with its stated values?

Chapter Four

Keeping It Lean:
The Nimble Church

The newspaper industry hit hard times in 2009. Several large metropolitan papers, including the *Seattle Post-Intelligencer* and the *Rocky Mountain News*, ceased circulation. The Tribune Company, which publishes the *Chicago Tribune*, the *Los Angeles Times*, and the *Baltimore Sun*, is in bankruptcy. Still other companies are staring into an uncertain future. As circulation numbers and advertising revenues shrink, the consensus among newsmongers is that the future of the daily paper is on the Internet. But even the most seasoned news sources have yet to determine how to make online news profitable.

Meanwhile, as the old pros wring their hands over the future of print, one small operation on the West Coast is showing them how it's done. The Southern California-based

Voice of San Diego was awarded one of investigative reporting's most prestigious awards for its coverage of a local corruption scandal in 2009. And in that year of seemingly inevitable news industry decline, *Voice* expanded.

One factor contributing to the new site's success is its size. *Voice of San Diego* is run by a skeleton crew of only eleven employees. That makes it lean, agile, and responsive. But the brilliance of *Voice of San Diego* is not its size. What makes the site remarkable is its focus. The paper's leadership has strict specifications about what types of stories their publication will cover. "We made a determination a long time ago," explains Scott Lewis, the site's chief executive, "that we wouldn't cover anything unless we could do it better than anyone else or unless no one else was covering it."

Because the site is committed to covering unreported and underreported news of local interest, the editors are satisfied with minimal output. So you won't find on their site features that most people—including news purveyors—consider essential to news outlets. "We don't worry about having a reporter covering the weather," Lewis says. "Somebody else already does that." And they pay little attention to popular news items in the human interest category. "We don't need to have somebody covering the panda birth at the zoo," Lewis continues, "because the three TV stations are all over that."[1]

This strategy has served them well. Every paper in San Diego received the same tip that led the *Voice* to uncover the local corruption scandal that earned the site its award. But only *Voice* followed up. The other papers were too busy covering the weather and welcoming panda cubs into the world.

With its lean, focused business strategy, *Voice of San Diego* has abandoned the conventional business wisdom of previous decades, which put a premium on diversity and expansion. Because it was increasingly difficult to please all of the people all of the time, companies chose to diversify into niche markets. There was safety in the shotgun approach. If one brand or product line failed, a company had others that would make up the loss.

In the emerging economy, though, corporations are beginning to recognize that size and diversification are potential liabilities. As I'm writing this, General Motors has recently streamlined its operations to focus on its four strongest brands. Like many corporations, GM is realizing what the *Voice of San Diego* has known all along: It requires a great deal of coordination, communication, and overhead to sail a large business through a capricious economy. In a digital age, the race is to the swift; today being small and focused is the key to business success.

ALL THINGS TO ALL PEOPLE

I have launched and led and languished through a host of church programs—both as a pastor and as a volunteer. My experience suggests that many churches live and die by them. We have learned from the business world that to thrive in ministry, we must diversify and multiply our ministry reach, and we usually do that through a multiplicity of programs.

We use programs to draw people into our fellowship. Church-growth literature promises success for the church that runs dynamic children and youth ministries, a network of small groups, recovery programs, and other activities and services that are age and stage-of-life specific. More programs and niche-market ministry means broader ministry reach. If one area is unsuccessful, there is always another branch of outreach that extends help to prospective church members.

Once people are in our churches, we get them involved by making sure they participate in or even lead our programs. Their participation becomes the way we judge how dedicated and mature they are. If they're engaged in our programs, we call them committed.

Programs can even become a means by which we judge our effectiveness as ministers—we can know we're doing a lot for Jesus if we're running a long list of successful activities.

Unfortunately, success in the heavily programmatic church depends upon a great deal of money and volunteer support. Programs become a line item or a page in the church budget that can leech valuable financial and human resources from the congregation. In an effort to be all things to all people, program-heavy congregations can find themselves in the same predicament as large, diversified corporations—they can be too bulky to be responsive and, in lean times, too large to be self-sustaining. If we aren't careful, the congregation becomes nothing more than a means of supporting the church's programming.

What would it look like if our churches took a page, appropriately modified, from the *Voice of San Diego*'s playbook and limited the number of programs and ministries we offer, focusing on one or two ministries that we can do particularly well? Imagine the difference if we approached church programming with this motto: "We won't run a program unless we are particularly gifted and equipped to run it or unless no one else is doing it."

Thinking of church programs in this way is a mark of the strategically small church that is liberated from the constant pressure to do more. But it requires rejecting the business model of church that has dominated the ministry imagination since the 1970s.

McCHURCH—I'M LOVIN' IT!

Attend any of the most popular ministry conferences today, and you will find that pastors and theologians share the platform with CEOs, marketers, and other market-savvy businesspersons. In some cases, these secular business leaders are not Christians; they don't have to be. The event coordinators do not invite them to share biblical wisdom or spiritual insight on pastoral care. They are simply asked to offer their advice on sound leadership and organizational principles.

The reason for this is simple. The prevailing assumption in ministry literature for the past few decades has been that all organizations—whether universities, corporations, or churches—are essentially the same. The principles that lead to success in one type of organization will yield the same results in the others. To be an effective minister, then, a pastor doesn't need to focus on theology or spiritual formation nearly as much as he should master the latest developments in organizational leadership.

This transition has had significant consequences for the

role of pastor. Pastor and church consultant Reggie McNeal describes this shift well:

> The church growth movement presented a steep learn-
> ing curve to church leaders. Ministers who had studied
> theology, biblical exegesis, and other subjects in classical
> seminary education now signed up for marketing semi-
> nars and business courses, subscribed to the Harvard
> Business Review, and joined the American Management
> Association.[2]

A pastor, in this way of thinking, is not so much a spiritual guide as he is a CEO of a growing organization. And many pastors are OK with that. One influential pastor believes we should abandon the metaphor of *shepherd* from our ministry vocabulary altogether. "That word needs to go away," he says. "It was culturally relevant in the time of Jesus, but it's not culturally relevant anymore."[3]

In place of the dour and introverted churchmen of the past, church as a corporation requires a charismatic CEO-type leader to cast and carry out the corporate vision, and it survives on a steady diet of financial and human resources. This is no doubt one reason why there are so relatively few "successful" (large) churches in America. Running a booming business requires a specific set of talents and abilities that most people, including most pastors, don't possess—marketing savvy, a superabundance of charisma, and a mind for corpo-rate structures and procedures.

When pastors become business managers, two significant things happen. First, they must begin to think of members and outsiders as customers and clients. Corporate literature sensitizes the pastor to the fact that his success depends on his ability to give his clientele what they are looking for. He knows that he is competing for people's attention with Disney and Marvel and Sunday afternoon football. Customers are aware of their needs and whether or not his organization is meeting them, and so is he.

Second, as the pastor begins to conceive of his target audience as consumers, church members and seekers can begin to understand themselves in the same terms. The church can easily lose sight of its mission to proclaim the gospel of God's redemption through Christ and become just one more organization competing for its piece of the market and vying for consumer loyalty. Would-be members begin to expect the church to meet their needs. When it doesn't, they take their attendance and tithes and volunteer support elsewhere.[4]

Longtime small-church pastor and author Eugene Peterson calls this "the Americanization of [the] congregation," which turns "each congregation into a market for religious consumers, an ecclesiastical business run along the lines of advertising techniques, organizational flow charts, and energized by impressive motivational rhetoric."[5]

In this environment, church programming is a logical solution. It offers us a tangible and manageable means of meeting people's needs and attracts them to our church. It provides a quantifiable way of measuring our effectiveness.

This is a fairly negative view of church programming, and I admit I'm overstating the case. Nevertheless, it is important to be aware that in some circles, particularly among younger church leaders, the term *church programs* has become an epithet for all that is wrong with the institutional church.

For a generation hungry for authenticity and community, "programs" feel staged, impersonal, and cold. They reek of institutionalism, bureaucracy, and insensitivity to human need.

For these folks, programming seems to privilege the organization over the congregation. "We're about people, not programs," they say. But in the end programs are not the problem, because people and programs are not mutually exclusive. There is a way to think about programming that is actually pro-people.

LET THERE BE PROGRAMS

The book of Acts gives us a clear vision for how programs that are pro-people should be selected and run.

Acts 6 opens with a problem: "In those days when the number of disciples was increasing, the Grecian Jews among them complained against the Hebraic Jews because their widows were being overlooked in the daily distribution of food."

Until this point in the story, the apostles had preached to massive crowds and seen thousands accept the gospel. They had healed the sick and crippled and served as midwives for the first Christian community. Sure, they had run up against external obstacles in the form of persecution from Jewish leaders, and they had witnessed God's judgment of the unfaithfulness of Ananias and Sapphira. But now, even as "the number of disciples was increasing," the fledgling Christian community was facing a trial that put its unity at risk. The early church's response to this challenge gives us a clear outline of how programming should work.

Begin With Need

The church's first program began with a legitimate need in the community: hungry widows. These early Christians understood that caring for widows was a gospel imperative (James 1:27; Deuteronomy 24:19). In order to show their widows proper care, they had already formalized their response into a "daily distribution of food"—a proto-program, at least.

But it wasn't working. This breakdown in the church's ministry led to an overhaul in the distribution procedure. The important thing to recognize is that the program was motivated by a community need: Some of the widows were being overlooked. This wasn't a church-growth strategy aimed at appealing to the Grecian widow demographic. Moreover, their need wasn't simply a felt need; it was theologically legitimate. The gospel compelled the church to find a solution to the problem.

Find Gifted Laypeople

Once the church identified the need, the apostles realized they needed to appoint gifted men to oversee it. The text makes it clear that though the care of widows was important, it would have been a distraction for the apostles who were supposed to serve the Word, not tables. To free themselves from the duty, the apostles suggested that the program be spearheaded by seven capable men whom the church recognized as "full of the Spirit and wisdom." Presumably, these were men who would have recognized the gospel mandate to care for the powerless and were mature enough to avoid becoming part of the problem by adding to the bickering and gossip.

Spread the Gospel

This short story ends triumphantly. The writer of Acts tells us that because of the church's attention to the widow problem, "the word of God spread." In fact, "The number of disciples in Jerusalem increased rapidly."

The Bible doesn't tell us exactly why this initiative resulted in the growth of the church. I suspect there were three reasons, at least. First, with the apostles free to dedicate themselves to the Word of God and prayer, the Word spread through their proclamation. Second, this program reinforced and illustrated one of the key virtues of the first church—it was marked by a profound unity and interdependence, even across racial and ethnic divisions. While the apostles preached the gospel with words, the church demonstrated the gospel through its programmed care for the widows in its midst. Finally, what better spokespeople could there be than the widows who have been provided for by the congregation? No doubt these women became a living testimony to their friends and family of the wonderful things that God had done for them through the church.

I can't speak for you, but the churches I have been a part of have not always been so selective with their programming. Instead of limiting our ministries to services that are theologically justifiable, we feel obligated to run certain programs because people expect that every legitimate church runs them. We run the programs the church growth specialists insist will result in the numerical growth of our organization.

Then, instead of finding folks to lead who are "full of the Holy Spirit and wisdom," we enlist any poor sucker with a pulse and a guilt complex to oversee a program they feel no real commitment to. I have recruited such volunteers. I have been that volunteer. When we burn through enough volunteers, the staff takes over the program, which keeps them from their primary responsibilities, not least of which are the ministry of the Word and prayer.

And instead of leading to the expansion of the kingdom, programs selected and run this way tend to use people up, overtax the staff, and result in exhaustion, bitterness, and a lack of resources.

Instead of running programs in this way, it may be wise to combine the pattern from Acts 6 with the insight from *Voice of San Diego*. Then the selection process for a new church program (or the decision about whether to throw out an existing program) would include answering these questions:

1. Does the program meet a legitimate community need?

2. Do we have qualified and interested people to oversee it, so that the leadership can be committed primarily to "the Word and prayer"?

3. Will it result in the spreading of the Word and the growth of the kingdom?

4. Is anyone else in our broader community already meeting this need?

5. Are we uniquely gifted to address it?

I suspect that if we were to hold our current programming up against this criteria, we would find that many of the programs we offer are unnecessary at best and, at worst, a harmful parasite of valuable resources.

THE STRATEGICALLY LEAN CHURCH

A church of any size can limit the number of its programs, and probably should. But this conversation is particularly good news for smaller churches. It can be incredibly liberating to realize that you no longer need to feel obligated to run a litany of programs for which you are under-resourced and understaffed. Instead, you can embrace the strategic advantage of running lean.

A smaller congregation can benefit from learning to value depth over volume. Instead of feeling obligated to provide a recovery group for divorcees and a meeting place for Alcoholics Anonymous and a day care and a focused ministry for twenty-somethings and a midweek children's program, churches can leverage their strengths by being selective about their ministry offerings. Like the *Voice of San Diego*, they can channel their limited resources into a smaller number of programs and potentially do these few things with greater depth and effectiveness.

Fortunately, many strategically small churches are already working under this perspective on programming, giving us great examples to emulate.

Redeemer Presbyterian Church (PCA) in Newport Beach, California, is a smaller congregation that is full of creative people. Situated in predominately business-oriented Orange County, the church attracts artists, musicians, and other culture makers. And Redeemer has found a way to maximize the talents of its creative laity.

The church runs a few typical ministries and programs, all of which they feel they can do particularly well. Because they have plenty of artistic types, for example, Redeemer puts considerable energy into its Sunday worship service. They also run a small-group program.

But the heart of Redeemer's ministry is what Pastor Jim Belcher calls the church's "Shalom ministries." The inspiration for these initiatives is Jeremiah 29:7. There, in his letter to the exiled remnant in Babylon, the prophet tells the Israelites to "seek the peace and prosperity of the city to which I [the Lord] have carried you into exile. Pray to the Lord for it, because if it prospers, you too will prosper." Taking these instructions to heart, Redeemer runs a host of events that emphasize cultural creation and engagement and bring the congregation into conversation with their Newport Beach neighbors. These events include worldview lectures and seminars (in which Redeemer pastors debate and discuss important issues with other religious leaders), art nights, and salons for deep discussion about cultural and theological issues. Most recently, Redeemer's commitment to culture creation has led them into dialogue with the local city council about the need for sacred space in new urban planning projects.

Obviously this sort of program wouldn't be effective everywhere. But Orange County is home to lots of educated people who care about culture, making Redeemer's effort relevant in their context. More important, the congregation is filled with folks who are uniquely gifted to oversee these sorts of projects.

To pursue these cultural engagements, Redeemer keeps a lean program schedule. They don't run midweek Bible studies at the church and haven't developed men's and women's programs. Instead, they focus all biblical study, discipleship, and leadership training through the community groups, and much of their outreach through their Shalom ministries. This allows the church to be intentional about spiritual formation, new leader development, and outreach without the burden of overhead costs and excessive strain on volunteers.

Eleven years ago, Edgewater Baptist Church in Chicago felt called to reach out to its community by meeting a neighborhood need. As is often the case in urban contexts, there were plenty of needs to be met. The Edgewater neighborhood houses a large gay community, is the American home of a large population of Bosnian refugees, and faces the challenges of homelessness.

Given its size—around 130 members—the church realized it needed to focus on only one of these issues. There were already a couple of gay outreach programs in the area and a Bosnian church plant in the neighborhood. One important need that wasn't being addressed by anyone else was the lack of child care for less affluent neighbors. The children of working parents had nowhere to go after school until the end of the workday. So Edgewater Baptist started Safeplace, an afterschool program and summer day camp that provides space and time for kids to do their homework, play games, and learn about abstinence, nutrition, and other practical health and safety issues.

The church subsidizes most of the program costs; parents pay what they can and no one is turned away for financial reasons. A handful of part-time staff members oversees operations. The church's decision to subsidize tuition and pay staff—when its budget only allows for a two-pastor staff—has demanded that the church intentionally streamline its programs. Safeplace is Edgewater Baptist's single major ministry.

The commitment has paid off. The church has between 120 and 130 worshipers on a given Sunday. But over 120 kids regularly attend Safeplace during the school year, and there are even more in the summer day camp. Edgewater Baptist's outreach through Safeplace has changed the congregation for the better. They are more multiethnic now than they were when the program began. Many of the church's youth are Safeplace graduates who attend the church even without their parents.

Together, these illustrations from Redeemer Presbyterian and Edgewater Baptist highlight a couple of the strengths of the smaller congregation for this sort of streamlined and innovative ministry.

First of all, pastors in smaller churches can be more intimately involved in the lives of their parishioners, and it is in the intimacy of those relationships that creative ideas emerge. Jim Belcher believes it is the "synergy between the people's heart and the pastor's heart" that produces the ministries that characterize his Redeemer congregation. He has a passion for cultural engagement, but it was individual members of the congregation that developed many of their most innovative programs. "When a pastor is close to his people," he explains, "he can know what they are passionate about." This is almost impossible in a larger church.

Pastors of strategically lean churches listen to their

congregation's stories and look for patterns. Does a significant number of people share a common narrative—whether deliverance from an addiction, recovery from abuse, or a history of unbelief or intellectual rebellion? Does a significant percentage of your congregation work in the same career—whether education, medicine, or manufacturing?

If several of your church members work at a nearby school and others feel compelled to ensure the quality of education for the children in your neighborhood, perhaps your church's unique ministry could focus on adopting the local school and providing mentors, tutors, and scholarships for extracurricular activities. If a majority of your congregation works at the local mill, perhaps your church should consider providing whatever support is necessary and unique to the people in that profession. Speaking practically, if the ministry initiative is launched as a result of congregational vision, there is a greater likelihood that members will support it with their time, money, and participation.

Second, in contrast to large regional churches, smaller, leaner churches can be more intimately aware of and responsive to the needs of their host communities. Safeplace did not arise out of a sense of the church's abilities and giftedness as much as from awareness of needs in the neighborhood.

Large churches are often regional rather than community based. They attract people from a broad geographical area, so they appeal to a particular demographic and draw people out of their communities to a central location. This can render them less sensitive to the needs of their immediate neighbors. Jim Belcher recognizes, for example, that Redeemer's cultural engagement is nothing that a large church couldn't do. "A big church may have the resources to do this sort of thing," Jim acknowledges. "But I don't think a big church would have the vision for it." Small churches, by contrast, can implant themselves in a community and become part of the local fabric.

PROGRAMS AND PARTICIPATION

One honest objection to this way of thinking about church programming is that it could conceivably limit the opportunities for congregational participation. If you only run one or two programs or ministries and someone's gifting doesn't equip him to participate, how can he be involved in the church's mission?

Limiting the number of ministry initiatives your church offers does not have to limit the ways the members of a small congregation can engage their community. Rick McKinley, pastor of Imago Dei Community in Portland, Oregon, is determined to limit the number of programs his church oversees. He does everything he can to keep from launching a ministry. If a church member approaches him about beginning an outreach to the homeless (for example), he encourages her first to find out if other churches or organizations in town are already ministering to the homeless. If there is already a vibrant ministry nearby, he encourages his members to join the effort as an ambassador of Imago Dei and, more important, of Christ. If a need is going unmet in the city, then Imago Dei will consider launching a program. But like the *Voice of San Diego*, they only put their efforts where no one else is working.

Instead of limiting a church's ministry reach, this approach can extend it. If a church were committed to joining existing outreach efforts, a congregation of 100 members could conceivably be involved in fifteen or twenty area ministries without the church's being financially responsible for any of them. Participation in outside organizations also facilitates relationships and cooperation between people within the congregation and people outside of it. This communicates to the community at large that a congregation is *for* them and eager to help, and is not just involved in ministry to aggregate members and create a larger organization. Something as simple as attending the local ministerial alliance or city council meetings can put a pastor in touch with how others are already meeting community needs.

Joining an existing ministry also helps a church keep the left hand from knowing what the right hand is doing. Rick McKinley says this is one motivation for reducing the number of programs at Imago Dei Community. His staff operates under the mantra "No logo, no ego." The church can be involved in ministry across the city without taking the credit for their good deeds.

MAKING THE HARD CHOICES

Running a lean calendar is not easy, especially if this hasn't been your church's historical strategy. If you've always offered twelve different Sunday school classes, a midweek children's outreach, a soup kitchen, a men's pancake breakfast, and so on, it will be difficult to trim your programming without offending someone. The leaders of each ministry often take great pride of ownership, even if they have to beg and plead for volunteers to help them week after week. And there are people who can't imagine the Tuesday morning

Bible study being held on Wednesday morning, let alone not at all. So it would be tempting to allow these programs to continue until they run out of steam on their own. But it might be wise instead to have some honest conversations about where resources would be best used. Even if ministry leaders are disappointed in the short run, in the long run it will be more energizing for everyone to be able to participate in a thriving ministry, regardless of whether or not it is run by your congregation.

On the other hand, some program leaders may be waiting for you to give them permission to stop what they are doing and look for another outlet for their time and talents. These quiet, faithful leaders would keep plugging away at their tasks, regardless of the results, simply because they are dutiful servants. Giving them a guilt-free "out" may be a tremendous boost to them and to your congregation.

COMPETITION VS. COOPERATION

A final advantage partnership offers a small church is the opportunity to favor cooperation over competition. There are many reasons one local church might compete with other local churches for visitors and members or refuse to partner with religiously unaffiliated social programs. Some of the reasons are justifiable. A church might be hesitant to work with a secular or municipal organization for fear that they would not be allowed to verbally share the gospel with the people they were serving. This is a legitimate concern, although in actual fact Christians are usually free to share their faith when they work with secular agencies, so long as they don't require people to sit through an evangelistic presentation before they receive whatever services the agency is offering. For example, you can't tell folks, "We'll be happy to vaccinate your children, if you'll first read this tract about the four spiritual laws."[6]

A church might also be hesitant to cooperate with another local congregation for theological reasons. You might be concerned, for example, that if a person attends another church they won't hear the gospel preached in its fullness. I respect that concern, although it can be overblown. No one ever said it explicitly, but the general sense in the church I grew up in was that all the other churches in our region that were not members of the same denomination were apostate. For us, cooperation with other churches was simply out of the question.

While there are legitimate reasons for avoiding cooperation, all too often the reason churches don't work together is because we have no idea what kinds of ministry are going on outside our church walls. It can be easy to believe that if our church isn't doing something, no one is.

This point was brought home to me not long ago. My colleague Skye Jethani and I met several local pastors for lunch to discuss what topics and challenges they would like to see us address in upcoming issues of *Leadership* journal. Not surprisingly, given our context in Chicagoland, the conversation drifted to the unique challenges of urban ministry. One pastor of a large church in the area explained that his congregation was planning to plant a new church in one of Chicago's most ethnically diverse neighborhoods. He was thrilled, if a little overwhelmed, about the possibilities of multiethnic ministry. They had just secured the purchase of an abandoned church building and were planning to start services soon. "There's just so much ministry potential in that area," he said. "That neighborhood really needs a good church."

Across the table, one of the other pastors chimed in. "We've been in that neighborhood for seven years," he said. "And we tried to buy that same church building, but you outbid us."

As you might imagine, that created a very awkward moment.

It's sad to me that neither of these pastors had ever met before our lunch. They were ministering in the same neighborhood and competing over the same facility. Their efforts could have been doubly effective if, instead of working against each other, they had found a way to work together.

This is just one example of how several churches in one neighborhood may have compatible visions for outreach, offer the same programs and ministries, and essentially compete with other local churches for a finite number of visitors and potential members. Choosing to limit your own church's programming schedule will force you to be more aware of how God is already at work in the efforts of other churches and organizations in the area and find ways to get on board.

CONCLUSION

It's thrilling to imagine the combined ministry opportunities in a city or region with a number of small churches each focusing their efforts on a different need in the community. Though individually their potential for impact may be limited to a single need or demographic, together they could do what no large church can do—extend the love of Christ down every avenue and boulevard in town.

This means, once again, that we must recognize and acknowledge that God is at work even when and where our church is not. The kingdom of God is larger than each of our churches; indeed, it is larger than all of our churches. Being strategically lean demands that we choose participation and cooperation over accumulation and competition.

This should be liberating for small churches. It's easy to believe that your church is at a disadvantage because it can't offer a full schedule of programs. I hope the examples in this chapter demonstrate that a lean calendar is actually a strategic advantage.

In the end, leveraging the strength of nimble and focused ministry requires a great deal of participation and leadership from within the congregation. A single pastor couldn't do it if the congregation expected the pastor to lead everything. Neither could a multiple-minister staff, if they hoped to keep their sanity. Ministering in this way means putting a great deal of confidence in the concept of the priesthood of every believer. But to address that more fully, we need another chapter.

Questions for Reflection for Pastors or Leadership Teams

1. Take some time to make a complete list of the programs your church runs—every last one of them. Highlight the ones you run just because you feel like you have to. How important are these programs to your church's ministry?

2. What programs are you running in your church that you know other nearby churches are also running?

Brainstorm three or four ways in which you might be able to partner with another local church so that the two of you are cooperating and not competing.

3. What needs do your neighbors (and church members) have that are not currently being met? Brainstorm three or four ways your church might be able to address those needs.

4. Think about the people who make up your congregation. What do they have in common? What passions do they share? What ministry is your church uniquely gifted to do?

Chapter Five

The Work of the People:
The Equipping Church

Imagine for a moment that you are part of the perfect church (I'm sure you've done this before). The congregation is made up of 100 adults, and because it is the perfect congregation, everyone serves in church-related ministries, giving five hours of leisure time per week. That's enough time for Sunday morning activities, a midweek program, and something like a committee meeting. At that rate, your spectacular congregation can log 500 volunteer hours in a given week. That's a level of participation that would tempt the saintliest of pastors to envy.

It's safe to assume that most of those 100 adults have jobs, and many of them have children. If they all work full time, they will spend a combined 4,000 hours on the job every week. And it is likely that they will spend another 500 hours or more serving on the PTA, coaching T-ball, playing golf, or volunteering with a local community organization.

Program-based ministry is designed to take place during people's extra time. We ask church members to donate their free evenings and weekends to the work of ministry. But even if we were to serve in a remarkable congregation in which every adult volunteered regularly, the amount of time people could spend as ministry participants is a miniscule percentage of the time they spend as employees, employers, stay-at-home moms or dads, coaches, den leaders, and volunteers. And the amount of spare time the average person has is shrinking.

Young couples today are strapped with considerably greater education and housing costs than were their parents and grandparents. Futurist Tom Sine estimates that the Greatest Generation spent roughly 30 percent of a single income on rent or mortgage; that same expense costs Gen-Xers 50 percent of two incomes. The average American is also working ten hours more per week than he was fifteen or twenty years ago. What this means for the church, in Sine's estimation, is that "young people will have less time for family, church, prayer, Scripture reading, witness, and service."[1] In other words, if people are working longer hours and spending more of their income on basic necessities, they are less and less likely to have disposable time or money to give the church.

Despite the fact that Americans are feeling greater demands on their time and money, they remain relatively generous. The National Conference on Citizenship reported in July 2009 that the number of volunteers in community agencies actually increased during the economic recession that began in late 2008.[2] It is easy for church leaders to consider their members uninvolved if they are not participating in church activities.

But it's very likely that their members are actively engaged somewhere. Instead of trying to get people into our facilities and programs five hours a week, we would do well to equip them to serve where they are the other fifty or sixty, to help them recognize their regularly scheduled activities and interests as potential ministry opportunities.

As we discussed in the previous chapter, strategically small churches streamline their programming by putting their energy and resources into ministries that they are particularly qualified to run or by addressing needs that other churches are leaving unmet. But this is only half the story. When it comes to ministry and outreach, strategically small churches have another advantage over their larger counterparts. Small church pastors can know their congregations deeply and intimately. They can discover the passions that drive the people in their pews. And they can equip their congregants to turn these passions into opportunities to advance the mission of God where they spend the bulk of their time and energy during the week.

MINISTRY MIDWIVES

For nearly forty years, the majority of the ministry at Altadena Baptist Church has been done by laypeople equipped to serve out of their gifts and passions. On the Sunday morning that Pastor George VanAlstine preached in view of a call at Altadena Baptist in 1972, he chose as his text Paul's teaching in Romans 12:4-5 on spiritual gifting: "Just as each of us has one body with many members, and these members do not all have the same function," Paul wrote, "so in Christ we who are many form one body, and each member belongs to all the others." Pastor VanAlstine went on to preach, as Paul instructed, that everyone is to serve cheerfully and with all their heart in the power of the Holy Spirit. Altadena Baptist accepted the challenge.

When I spoke to George and his co-pastor, Connie DeVaughn, just weeks before the church's seventy-fifth anniversary celebration, they were preaching through Romans 12 once again. "Our ministry has always grown out of where the members are in their passions and their relationships with God," explains Connie, who joined George on staff in 1991. "That's been intentional on our part; but the fact is, because we're small, it's also been a necessity. We wouldn't have gotten anything done otherwise."

Encouraging members to serve out of their passions and gifts has many strategic advantages. The first is that it multiplies ministry opportunities exponentially. If a church's programming is determined by a single pastor or even a pastoral staff, the ministries the church offers are likely to reflect the gifts and passions of the leadership. If, on the other hand, the ministry develops out of the interests of the congregation, the Spirit can lead in surprising directions.

About twenty-five years ago, an Altadena Baptist member named Paul felt led to organize a Black History Month celebration as an outreach event. The church had committed in the early 1970s to being a congregation that would reflect the changing demographics in the neighborhood around the church. Several years later, when the church's African-American population was well established, a Black History Month celebration seemed an appropriate tribute to the congregation's work for racial reconciliation. The first celebration more than two decades ago was organized by one motivated layperson. Today, the annual celebration is the church's largest outreach event. People from a number of other churches, leaders from the Black community, and influential political leaders from the Pasadena area attend every year.

For these twenty-five years, the celebration has been led entirely by laypeople. "We have been very careful not to take over planning the event," George reflects. As far as George and Connie are concerned, if the event had not begun in the heart of a church member, it never would have begun at all. "The celebration is something we wouldn't have thought of doing," says George. "Even if we had, we wouldn't have had the guts to do it."

More recently, a man named Matt came to George and Connie with a passion for evangelism. Matt is not a great public speaker. He doesn't deliver a stirring testimony. He's not comfortable talking to strangers about Jesus. But he is certain the church should be active in sharing the gospel. Connie helped Matt recognize that the point at which his passion for evangelism and his talents for athletics intersect is a field ripe for spiritual harvest. As a result, the twenty-something P.E. teacher single-handedly arranged for Altadena Baptist to play a significant role in the annual Los Angeles marathon, an event that provides an extraordinary opportunity for relational evangelism.

Throughout the year, Matt regularly contacts Connie with other outreach ideas that would never have occurred to her. "Most of them involve sports," she observes, "which doesn't do a lot for me personally. But the vision and energy are his, so I help make his ideas a reality."

As these examples suggest, George and Connie think of themselves essentially as midwives to ministry at Altadena

Baptist. They let the passions of the people in their congregation spawn the majority of ministry ideas. But they recognize that they have an active role in that process. During our conversation, the co-pastors identified several important ways they help equip their members to minister from their gifts.

Their first important function is to help church members identify their gifts and interests. Often people are eager to be involved in the ministry and outreach of the church, but they have no idea where and how they want to serve. Part of the pastor's role is to help them find the place where their gifts can best be used for the greater good.

Second, pastors are responsible for what George calls the "function of testing reality." Church members have lots of great ideas for ministry, but some of them are simply unrealistic. The pastor's role in these situations is to let his experience provide perspective as a parishioner tries to sharpen his or her vision for ministry. Often this means redirecting someone's energy in a more productive direction.

Third, George and Connie function as advocates for their members' ministry ambitions. "Once we buy in to the idea, the congregation follows," George says. It is important to them that no one does anything alone. So the pastors present their parishioners' ideas to the congregation to give people a chance to offer feedback and volunteer to join the endeavor.

Fourth, the pastors realize that they provide a theological filter for program materials and the messages of evangelistic events. A pastor's training and education may make him more sensitive than the average church member to matters of theological content. And ultimately the pastor is responsible for the message church members carry into the community.

Finally, when a ministry initiative has the support of the

congregation, George and Connie become facilitators who provide whatever support, council, or training may be necessary to ensure the ministry's success.

For Altadena Baptist Church, equipping the saints for ministry through investing in their spiritual formation and letting the church's programs develop out of their passions has resulted in greater kingdom impact.

HIGH-ACCOUNTABILITY/LOW-CONTROL MINISTRY

Trinity Lutheran Church in Lynnwood, Washington, is another church committed to letting ministry bloom out of the gifts of its members.

When Pastor Eileen Hanson joined the Trinity staff in 2006, she helped move the church away from exclusive dependence upon "pillar ministries," such as choir, Sunday school, and weekend worship, and diversified the church's ministry into smaller, organic expressions called Mustard Seed initiatives.

"Mustard Seed is not so much a program as an attitude," Eileen explains. "It's an effort to put into practice the biblical principle of the priesthood of all believers." While her pastoral responsibilities at Trinity are fairly traditional, her relationship to Mustard Seed is different. She serves as a coordinator and mentor for Mustard Seed ministry small-group leaders, ensuring that each of them accomplishes the discipleship requirements: (1) nurturing an upward relationship with the Triune God by engaging Scripture; (2) nurturing an inward relationship with others for fellowship and support; and (3) nurturing an outward relationship with neighbors near and far through invitation and service.

Beyond this level of oversight, each group is autonomous—free to interpret and apply these principles through their own particular interests.

Eileen calls this high-accountability/low-control ministry. It is high accountability because the pastor is ultimately responsible for the church's theology, the message its members are proclaiming, and the general success of the church in accomplishing its core mission to spread the gospel to the ends of the earth.

But it is low control because, as Eileen explains, "The responsibility for reaching out into the community is primarily the congregation's, not mine. My job is to make sure the leaders are equipped and supported." Eileen is concerned with ensuring *that* the gospel is being proclaimed in the community, but she has little control over *how* it is being done. "If you are truly equipping people, then you must mentor them, empower them—and then let them go."

Letting go may be the pastor's biggest challenge in this form of ministry. Most pastors are accustomed to high-accountability/high-control ministry. Not only are they responsible for the theology and mission of the church, but they often feel compelled to micromanage the means by which that mission is fulfilled. They teach their people to evangelize their neighbors, for example, and then offer them a script to use in conversation, suggest venues and situations in which evangelism is most likely to happen, or encourage their people to bring their friends to special evangelistic events at the church.

Eileen sees this common approach as counter to Jesus' method of sending out disciples. "The sending passages in the Gospels aren't about how much training you have or about using the right script," she says. "Ultimately, they are about being willing to carry the good news that the kingdom of God is near."

According to Eileen, high-accountability/low-control ministry is all about relationships. The underlying principle of this approach to ministry is that the work of the people inside and outside the church should be organic, not imposed by a programming professional. But for that strategy to work, the pastor must know her flock intimately. This intimacy begins with conversations, not strategic plans and a clear methodology.

Eileen advises pastors to begin talking to their people about their passions and interests. It may not be clear at first how a person's interests can be directed into a ministry opportunity. Nevertheless, take the time to imagine with your congregants how God could work through their interests or might already be at work in them. This might require an extended period of meeting, mentoring, and discipleship. Ultimately, though, this mentoring can work through the congregation in waves, as mentored members begin to mentor others in finding God at work in their gifts and passions.

"High-accountability/low-control ministry frees the imagination to recognize that ministry takes many different manifestations," Eileen says. For some church members, ministry remains informal—perhaps simply stopping over at a neighbor's house for tea. For others, combining their interests with a mission mindset results in full-fledged lay-run programming. "It's exciting to watch how enthusiasm spreads through a congregation when people begin to catch a vision for what one person can do when they minister from their gifts."

ENCOURAGING FULL PARTICIPATION

The most obvious benefit of letting ministry develop organically rather than programming it is that lay-developed ministry requires considerably fewer resources. Eileen says that all of Trinity's resources—including people, money, and facilities—are made available to the Mustard Seed small groups and their leaders. But because, for the most part, ministry is happening where people are already active, they require virtually no overhead.

A more profound benefit of organic ministry is that it breaks down all barriers to active participation. Staff-developed programs can actually exclude people from the work of the church. For example, programs tend to be age-specific so that people can only participate if they are in a certain stage of life. Or they might require a certain level of expertise or training. Others, especially evangelistic programs, are best suited to particular personality types. Still other programs can be particularly appealing to one ethnic group and seem insignificant to others. For example, I recently interviewed a multiethnic church staff for *Leadership* journal. One of the pastors, a first-generation American citizen from Mexico, said, "When we offer small groups the list fills up with white people. None of our members from other ethnicities understand what all the fuss is about."

But if people are expected simply to engage in ministry where they are currently active in the church or community, then they aren't kept from participating in God's mission because they lack proper training, experience, or credentials—or because they are too young. In fact, Trinity Lutheran and Altadena Baptist have both found that letting ministry develop organically increases opportunities for young people in their congregation. This is great news for the strategically small church that is also committed to intergenerational ministry. (There will be more on this in the next chapter.)

Altadena Baptist's Connie DeVaughn tells a great story about a young man in their church named Ben. Ben began approaching Connie with suggestions for improving the children's Sunday school program when he was in the fourth or fifth grade. Connie recalls that he had a seemingly endless list of ideas—and most of them were good. "My first thought," she said, "was that this kid is smart and he knows he's smart. And I was not inclined to encourage him." But she recognized a passion and energy in Ben and decided that instead of quelling it, she should channel it.

So she began taking his ideas seriously. His ideas for improving Sunday school were successful. When he was a little older, he initiated a peer youth group that studied the teachings of Jesus and then put them into practice. This last year, at only seventeen years old, Ben organized and administrated the church's Vacation Bible School program.

"It would have been easy to dismiss Ben's ideas because he's young," Connie admits. But with a little direction and correction from Connie, his ministry in the church has thrived. In fact, Connie credits Ben's active participation in ministry with keeping him in the church. A few years ago, Ben's brother left the congregation to attend a larger church with a vibrant youth program. She believes Ben has stayed because he's always been encouraged and listened to.

Eileen Hanson tells a similar story about a group of young girls from Trinity Lutheran. A few years ago, ten eleven-year-old girls formed what they called the Christian Drama Studio. The ensemble was made up of five girls who attended various churches (Trinity among them) and five who had no faith home. Their ministry to the Lynnwood, Washington, community was to rehearse plays (usually simplified versions of Bible stories) and perform them to senior adults in nearby assisted-living homes.

"Really, the girls were a bunch of divas that enjoyed the spotlight," Eileen says. But she decided to encourage them anyway. At first, the primary spiritual component of their meetings was a time of prayer at the beginning. Even this was superficial, Eileen recalled. "Eleven-year-old girls can pray about their pets for half an hour."

Over the years, though, and with Eileen's guidance, the group matured. The prayer time became deeper and more meaningful. Girls who were uninterested or unwilling to pray in the early days were now eager to lead the group's prayer times. Before long their response to a tragic accident would prove they had grown deep in their faith.

About three years after the group began, one of the girls was killed in an avalanche. The day after the accident, the Christian Drama Studio, whose members were now about fourteen years old, collected four prayer shawls that were knitted by another Mustard Seed group in the church. They took these to the grieving family and presented them, one at a time, to the mother, father, sister, and brother of their deceased fellow actor. They told the family that the shawls represented the prayers of God's people and the great grace of God that surrounds them in the midst of their pain.

Shortly thereafter, they assembled a group of grieving schoolmates who were troubled by serious questions following the death of their friend—was their friend in heaven or hell? Did God let this happen? And if so, why? The Christian Drama

Studio invited Eileen to moderate a conversation through which the girls and their pastor provided a safe place for hurting teens to ask difficult questions.

In a final act of ministry in the midst of tragedy, the girls organized a bake sale. The proceeds were donated to the search-and-rescue team that found their friend's body.

"The Christian Drama Studio began as a fairly self-indulgent group," remembers Hanson. But by meeting the girls in their passion and helping them find a way to put it to work for the kingdom, the girls became ambassadors for Christ. "In the end," Hanson says, "they extended comfort and hope to their peers, adults, even an entire neighborhood."

If equipping church members to minister from their gifts increases opportunities for young people to engage in God's mission, it is also a great way to connect with people on the fringes of your ministry who wouldn't ordinarily participate in a traditional program. George, Connie, and Eileen all acknowledge that they have met several people in their churches who never felt welcomed or engaged in other congregations because they never found a way to serve. What this communicates to some people on the margins is that they aren't good enough, that they don't have the right qualities for participating in church life. Engaging them personally and equipping them to serve where they are can bring these people from the margins to the center of church life.

PUTTING MISSION FIRST

Letting your ministry rest on the work of the people requires a significant shift of perspective.

The deep question at the heart of this conversation is how

we understand the relationship between the church as an organization and the church's mission. It is very easy to believe that our primary objective as church leaders is to grow a religious institution—to add members and enlarge our sphere of influence. If we understand our jobs in this way, mission becomes a means of church growth. Programming then becomes extremely attractive because it offers a quantifiable method of measuring our success.

What Altadena Baptist and Trinity Lutheran have both recognized is that mission is not a means of growing the church; mission is the church's purpose and goal. Equipping people to serve where they are—out of their gifting and passion—is a great way to advance the mission of God. But it's not necessarily a great way to grow an institution. It is difficult to measure our impact and success when we are not accumulating people into a few key ministries. In other words, equipping the saints for service outside the church privileges the mission over the institution. It acknowledges, as pastor and writer Alan Hirsch has said, that "although we frequently say 'the church has a mission'. . . a more correct statement would be 'the mission has a church.' "[3]

The apostle Paul goes to great lengths in his letters to communicate that accomplishing the mission of God is a team sport. Together, every congregation is the physical body of Christ on earth; individually, every person is an integral member of that body (1 Corinthians 12:27). In his infinite wisdom, the Holy Spirit has granted each person a unique gift and purpose within the congregation and for its common good (1 Corinthians 12:7). A healthy church is one in which the body is strengthened and built up because every member is serving his brothers and sisters and their broader community through his or her gifts (Ephesians 4:12).

PLAYING THE HAND YOU'RE DEALT

Focusing our energies on equipping people to serve from their passions requires other significant shifts in thinking. For one, it demands that churches recognize that pastors and laity are partners in ministry. It is often the case, particularly in smaller churches, that the congregation views its pastor as someone they have called to minister to them. "Small-church pastors have a lot of fingers in a lot of pies," says Connie DeVaughn. "Sometimes laypeople can feel that if the pastor doesn't attend or isn't a part of their ministry effort, then it isn't a 'real' ministry." It may take time for members of the congregation to begin to recognize themselves as the primary doers of ministry. Once that happens, the church will attract members new and old who are eager to be active but have not yet found their place.

On the other hand, many pastors are happy being the professional ministry coordinator. They trust their expertise and are hesitant to relinquish control of the church's mission into the congregation's hands. The risk of this sort of ministry is that a pastor can make disciples of himself instead of disciples of Jesus. Organic ministry will not work if a pastor insists on micromanaging his flock's ministry efforts.

An integral part of trusting your congregation is being confident that God has providentially brought the right people into your church at the right time. At Altadena Baptist, George and Connie believe that every person enters the church with something to *offer* the congregation and in need of something *from* the congregation. And believing that God brings the right people into the church at the right time means constantly reconsidering what your needs are.

"I have a bone to pick with God," Connie told me. "I have often asked him why he hasn't brought us the charismatic and gifted youth leader that will grow our youth ministry. I ask him why he hasn't given us somebody better than me." In the end, Connie recognizes that if God hasn't sent the right person to meet a need, then perhaps it isn't actually a need.

Letting ministry develop organically also means being willing to end or postpone ministries when they lose the congregation's support. Maintaining a program or ministry that no one will volunteer for is a sure sign that the church has elevated the needs of the organization over the call to mission.

Finally, if ministry is primarily the equipping of the saints to serve where they are, then church leaders will need to recognize that not all gifts and passions must be turned church-ward. Churches often make the mistake of "getting someone involved" in an internal ministry of their church, making it impossible for them to serve outside the church's walls and programming. Altadena Baptist knows this, and they make an effort to recognize people in the congregation who put their spiritual gifts and passions to work in ministries outside the church. Instead of redirecting what someone is doing, they want to baptize their venues of service. "There are times when we could use more of someone's energy in church-related events," Connie explains, "but we don't, because they are doing such great work in the community at large."

A LIBERATING LETDOWN

The focus of this chapter has been on getting people engaged and putting people to work. It's important to point out that our goal should not be to overburden people with individual ministry endeavors instead of programs. Every disciple passes through seasons of service and seasons of rest. While George, Connie, and Eileen all agree that a pastor's primary role should be to encourage and equip his or her people to minister from their gifts, they are quick to point out that from time to time people should be invited to simply retreat and recuperate. Ministering from our strengths is its own type of rest; it is a rest, at least, from the guilt or pressure of constant service for its own sake. But there are times when a true Sabbath is in order.

Finally, I should acknowledge that this sort of ministry can take place in congregations of any size. As similar as they are in philosophy, there is one important difference between the two churches I've highlighted in this chapter. Altadena Baptist has a little over 300 members. Trinity Lutheran has over 2,000. A church doesn't have to be small to do micro ministry. This illustrates the important point that letting your church's programming develop out of the strengths of its members is not just something small churches have to do because they don't have a choice. Rather, it's a strategic approach to ministry that extends a church's reach by getting more people involved at a grassroots level.

It is significant to point out, too, that this sort of ministry is not only practically advantageous. It is also profoundly biblical. During his earthly ministry, Jesus regularly preached to large crowds, but he communicated his most intense instruction through intimate personal relationships. Just as he made disciples, he commanded his followers to do the same. Likewise, the apostle Paul made an enormous impact for the kingdom through his letters. But he understood that his legacy would be transmitted primarily through his "spiritual sons," men like Timothy and Titus. That's why he encouraged them, also, to "entrust [his teachings] to reliable men who will also be qualified to teach others." It was through Jesus' disciples and Paul's spiritual sons that the gospel spread, and is still spreading, throughout the world.

High-accountability/low-control ministry plays to a strength of the small church, namely its relative intimacy. But just because this sort of ministry will be easier to accomplish in smaller churches than in larger ones, I don't mean to imply at all that it will be easy. Equipping the saints for the work of ministry requires a deep personal investment. Somehow, a church leader must get to know each member of his flock in order to assess their strengths and weaknesses. After helping them focus their attention on an appropriate ministry field, he must also train them and guide them toward more fruitful ministry. Just because the control is low doesn't mean the minister's involvement is minimal. This model is far more demanding. But the payoff is immeasurable for the church willing to become strategically small in the way it equips its people for the kingdom's sake.

Questions for Reflection for Pastors or Leadership Teams

1. Make a list of people in your congregation who have gifts and passions they are not currently able to use in your church's programming. How might you help them learn to minister from these gifts, either inside or outside the church?

2. How many members of your congregation already spend a significant amount of time in ministry outside the church walls? How can you make your support of their ministries more apparent?

3. What would have to change in order for your church to embrace this sort of organic ministry? Would the congregation resist? Would the staff? What do you see as the important first steps in this direction?

Chapter Six

New Focus on the Family:
The Intergenerational Church

Churches today face two daunting challenges when it comes to young people: attracting them and keeping them.

Twenty- and thirty-somethings have become notoriously difficult to reach (recall the story of Willow Creek's Axis ministry from chapter 2). The Southern Baptist Convention (SBC), the United States' largest Christian denomination, has reported a sharp decline in the number of 18-to-34-year-olds they have welcomed into the fold in the last twenty-five years. In 1980, SBC churches baptized over 100,000 young adults; in 2005, that number had fallen to around 60,000. This decline is even more precipitous given that it is happening at a time when the country's population is growing faster than ever. Lest this sound like an indictment of our Baptist brethren, it's important to note that they are not alone. According to the American Religious Identification Survey (ARIS) of 2008, every denomination has lost adherents in the past few years. The category of devotees that has grown the most is the "nones," people who claim no religious affiliation at all.[1]

As alarming as, if not more so than, the slowing rate of conversions nationwide is the rate at which American churches are losing their own kids. Statistics vary in the spate of recent books on the topic of church leavers, but conservative estimates indicate that at least 50 percent of church-attending teens will no longer be engaged in a local congregation by the time they reach their mid-twenties.[2] Many researchers put the dropout rate closer to 80 percent.

Nearly fifty years ago, Jim Rayburn, founder of Young Life, said, "It's a sin to bore a kid with the gospel." A majority of churches seem to agree. Since then the predominant strategy for reaching young people has been to offer age-specific ministries for children, teens, and young adults in which teaching is age-appropriate and the service styles are relevant, entertaining, and compelling. In one sense, the strategy has worked. We have given the people what they want. Sociologist Christian Smith reports in his book *Soul Searching* that teens are overwhelmingly content with the churches in which they grow up. In fact, Smith finds that 77 percent of churchgoing teens plan to attend the same sort of church they attend now when they are twenty-five years old.

Despite their intentions, though, a clear majority of them drift by the time they reach college. Smith says that the reasons they give for leaving aren't dramatic. "Many cannot explain their disengagement from religion," he says, "many seem simply to have drifted."[3] Thom and Sam Rainer state the matter more succinctly: "Churchgoing students drop out of the church because it is not essential to their lives."[4] We may give young people what they want. But it is clear that we have not given them what they need.

Small churches may feel the weight of this topic even more heavily than larger ones. Even as I write this, there are families in our church that are considering leaving because our children's and youth programming doesn't appeal to their kids. But some strategically small churches have discovered that the solution to the generation problem may be counterintuitive. Instead of providing more exciting age-specific ministries, they are finding hope by bringing the generations together.

FRIENDS AND FAMILY

A friend of mine is on staff at a mid-sized church that saw a spike in the number of college students attending several years ago. The staff found the surge perplexing, considering the church doesn't have a college ministry and wasn't equipped to provide one. My friend found a group of the students gathered after the service one Sunday morning and asked them what they expected from the church—if they hoped, for example, that the congregation would create a college ministry for them. One of the students surprised him with her answer. "We come here because you *don't* have a college ministry. We want to be part of the church." The students didn't want to be targeted for specialized ministry.

This response turns conventional church-growth wisdom on its head. Why would college students be attracted to a church that wasn't providing a ministry for them? One reason may be related to the way the emerging generation thinks of friends, family, and the church.

For ten years, beginning September 22, 1994, the television sitcom *Friends* articulated the ethos of one generation of viewers and influenced the worldview of the next. When the show began, its main characters—Ross, Rachel, Phoebe, Joey, Chandler, and Monica—were all in their mid-twenties, making them textbook representatives of Generation X. The series was wildly successful; the finale in 2004 was the second-most-watched television show of the year, coming in just behind the Super Bowl. If the burning pop-culture question for my parents' generation was "Who shot J.R.?" the unresolved quandary of mine was "Were Ross and Rachel *really* on a break?"

From the very beginning of the series, I recall pastors and other concerned Christians warning parents about the corrosive effects of the characters' morals on us impressionable young folks. Sex was a frequent topic of conversation on the show, and more often than not it was casual sex. One lead character, Ross, was married, divorced, and remarried three times during the show's ten-year run. And throughout the series, the show's writers consistently and intentionally undermined the traditional Christian understanding of marriage. There is a lesbian wedding in season two, in which the officiating minister explains, "Nothing makes God happier than when two people—any two people—come together in love."

Despite the show's questionable content, what resonated with many viewers (what resonated with me) was that the writers of *Friends* articulated the isolation many in my generation felt as a result of the disintegration of our families. Like the generation they represented, most of the friends on the show were the children of broken homes: Phoebe was an orphan; Chandler's parents divorced because his father was gay; Rachel's parents divorced in season two. Like I did with my own friends in high school and college, NBC's friends talked frequently about the scars they carried from the collapse of their biological families.

There is no denying that Christian critics were right. *Friends* actively and radically changed the definition of family. But the charge misses the point. The writers weren't motivated simply by a liberal or irreligious agenda. Rather, they presented life the way many of us experienced it. Because their own families were so dysfunctional, they created familial bonds where they could find them—in each other. Their definition of family extended well beyond the nuclear unit because their circumstances demanded that they understand family in functional terms. Family, the show communicated, is the people who are there for you when you need them. These people included ex-wives, half-siblings, and (most important) friends, the family you choose. A *Time* article titled "The 100 Best TV Shows of All Time," summarized the appeal of the show in this way:

> "[The show's] Gen-X characters were the children of divorce, suicide, and cross-dressing, trying to grow up without any clear models of how to do it. They built ersatz families and had kids by adoption, surrogacy, out of wedlock or with their gay ex-wives. . . . But the well-hidden secret of this show was that it called itself *Friends*, and was really about family."[5]

Ironically, despite the early resistance from many Christians, the show left its mark on the way we think about relationships. Today you can hear the theme song from *Friends* in youth-group worship services. This is just one more sign that the emerging generation of young adults is in a tireless pursuit of family. In *Lost and Found*, Ed Stetzer, *et al.*, reports that the younger churched and unchurched alike are "looking for mentors who are willing to invest in their lives and teach them some things along the way." This unparented and under-parented generation is eager to learn from other people's experiences and to hear words of wisdom from adults who have survived the challenges we are only beginning to face—marrying and starting a career and beginning families among them.

Not only that, young people are eager to be mentors, as well. Stetzer reports that young adults are "extraordinarily willing to invest themselves in the lives of those who are younger and have even less experience than they do. These younger adults," he continues, "are committed to providing for others what they hope will be provided for them."[6]

In other words, young people are not looking for another entertaining, age-specific worship experience. Instead they desperately desire a church that can offer them something they can find nowhere else in the world: a family. That is good news for the church with eyes to see; a family is just what the community of faith is called to be.

FAITH AND FAMILY IN THE BIBLE

In both the Old and New Testaments, the responsibility for the spiritual formation of the young rests on the older members of the worshiping community. In the Old Testament, the locus for religious education was, by and large, the biological family. This is because, unlike their children, the parents had been eyewitnesses to God's activity in the past. Moses tells the Israelites:

> Remember today that your children were not the ones
> who saw and experienced the discipline of the Lord your

> God: his majesty, his mighty hand, his outstretched arm;
> the signs performed and the things he did in the heart of
> Egypt, both to Pharaoh king of Egypt and to his whole
> country; what he did to the Egyptian army, to its horses
> and chariots, how he overwhelmed them with the waters
> of the Red Sea as they were pursuing you, and how the
> Lord brought lasting ruin on them . . . it was your own
> eyes that saw all these great things the Lord has done.
> (Deuteronomy 11:2–7)

There were no written Scriptures, no television documentaries, no flannelgraph Sunday school curricula. The only way the Israelite children would know that God's promise of faithfulness was extended to them was if their parents told them. And the primary way Israel transferred the faith to its children was by rehearsing with them the story of God's faithfulness.

Family and Faith in the Old Testament

Twice in the Old Testament, at pivotal moments in Israel's history, God establishes a lasting ceremony or memorial that provides a way for Israel to pass on the content of its faith to its children. The first is in Exodus 12. Following a detailed description of the Passover celebration, God tells Moses that this is to be a "lasting ordinance for you and your descendants." The ritual isn't an empty religious activity; it is a means of educating the nation's children in the story of their Savior's love. When the Israelite children ask, "What does this ceremony mean to you?" their parents are to tell them about God's deliverance from Egypt.

A similar thing happens when the Israelites cross the Jordan River to enter the Promised Land. Representatives from the twelve tribes each carry a stone into the Jordan, where they build a memorial to the Lord's faithfulness. Joshua explains, "In the future, when your children ask you, 'What do these stones mean?' tell them that the flow of the Jordan was cut off before the ark of the covenant of the Lord" (Joshua 4:6–7). In both cases, the forms of worship are meant to prompt questions. The narrative of God's redemption provides the answers. Israel's story of God's love was passed from parents to children.

Similarly, God also expected the parents in Israel to pass on the contents of the Law. Just after Moses delivers the Ten Commandments, he tells the people, "These commandments that I give you today are to be upon your hearts. Impress them on your children" (Deuteronomy 6:6–7). The Law is never divorced from the story of God's redemption. It is instruction by which the people will respond in gratitude to God's historical faithfulness.

Because the family was responsible for training its children in the faith, the venue for education was everyday life, not a classroom. Referring to the commandments of the Law, Moses instructs parents, "Talk about them when you sit at home and when you walk along the road, when you lie down and when you get up" (Deuteronomy 6:7–8). The family dwelling itself was the classroom, as the people were instructed to write the Law "on the doorframes of your houses and on your gates" (Deuteronomy 6:9).

Family Reimagined

In the New Testament, there are still no professionals dedicated to training young believers. Instead, the worshiping community continues to be responsible for the spiritual formation of its children. But starting with Jesus, the New Testament writers begin talking about family in broader terms.

Jesus expands the definition of *family* from one's immediate, biological relatives to include all who are knit together in faith. Once while Jesus was teaching in someone's home, his mother and brothers wanted to speak with him. When a messenger told him his family wanted to see him, Jesus "point[ed] to his disciples [and] said, 'Here are my mother and my brothers. For whoever does the will of my Father in heaven is my brother and sister and mother' " (Matthew 12:49–50).

The apostle Paul continues this emphasis in his epistles. Paul addresses the relationships of the generations in the church most directly in First Timothy and Titus. In both of these letters, Paul refers to his recipients as his sons in the faith (1 Timothy 1:2; Titus 1:4). Also, when Paul gives Timothy instructions regarding the relationships between church members, he exhorts him to think about his congregants in familial terms: "Do not rebuke an older man harshly," Paul says, "but exhort him *as if he were your father*. Treat younger men *as brothers*, older women *as mothers*, and younger women *as sisters*, with absolute purity" (1 Timothy 5:1–2, emphasis added). In the New Testament, "kingdom relationships are depicted as the believer's primary family."[7]

For Jesus and Paul, the responsibility for religious education still falls on the family, just as it did in the Old Testament. But the definition of *family* has been expanded. Paul's vision of church life in his letter to Titus includes every member encouraging and instructing the others to embody the gospel in their behavior. The older women are to teach the younger women "to love their husbands and children, to be self-controlled and pure, to be busy at home, to be kind, and to be subject to their husbands" (Titus 2:4–5). Older men are to encourage the younger men to be self-controlled, do good, and show integrity and seriousness (Titus 2:6–7). When these relationships operate appropriately, the young learn to live the gospel by the examples of their Christian "family," and the Christian community embodies the faith in such a way that outsiders take notice and God is glorified.

To a generation devastated by the fracturing of the biological family, the New Testament's concept of congregation as family brings a breath of hope. Diana Garland writes in her landmark book *Family Ministry*:

> The new model of family is not biological kinship but adoption. Sometimes our biological kinfolk desert and betray us. Sometimes our own life journeys take us far from kinfolk, or death separates us. . . . The church must follow Christ by ensuring that no one in the family of faith is familyless—that everyone is adopted into family. . . . The adoptive family has become the ideal, the model, the witness that there are no limits to God's ability to create goodness, not even the limits of biology.[8]

Unfortunately, in nearly every church I've been a part of, there has been little opportunity for children, teens, and young adults to learn their place in the body of Christ by interacting with older Christians. In the Scripture passages above, training in gospel living takes place in relationships. It involves older men instructing younger men in their behavior and older women leading younger women in holiness. By contrast, in the churches I've been a part of, nearly every teaching moment occurs in an age-specific context suited for transmitting information, whether it's a Sunday school classroom, a small-group Bible study, or a midweek educational program. These ministries are important, of course, but unless our churches find a way to bring the generations together in worship and service, I fear we are not providing the kind of training in righteousness that the New Testament has called us to provide.

A SURPRISING ADVANTAGE

Church leaders typically consider it a liability when they are unable to provide focused age-specific ministry to every demographic in the congregation. Providing excellent services and fellowship times for children and youth is a tried and true method for increasing church attendance. A pastor of a large church once explained the value of a strong children's ministry to me in these terms: "If you take the children by the hand, you have the parents by the throat." Youth groups, too, are essential for attracting and retaining church members. Because parents are rightly concerned that their teenage children have the right kind of friends and fear that their children will leave a church they find boring, many families head to larger churches with vibrant youth groups when their kids get to high school.

But the largest churches today are recognizing the weaknesses of age-segmented ministry. In large and thoroughly age-segregated churches where the generations seldom interact, children and youth can move through the church without ever being integrated into congregational life in any meaningful way. They go from the nursery to children's church and from children's church to youth group. Then after they graduate from high school, many of them head off to college where they don't know how to look for a worshiping community. So a growing number of larger churches is hiring personnel whose primary responsibility is to find ways to bring the generations together. Here again, small churches have the strategic advantage. Human nature dictates that most people gravitate toward people who are like themselves. In a church of 2,000 members, it is easy enough for teenagers to spend their time exclusively with teenagers, young parents to congregate only with other young parents, and older couples to gravitate toward other older couples. They can all remain in their separate spheres, rarely interacting with members of the other age groups. In a smaller church, however, this is nearly impossible. In a smaller church everyone is more naturally aware of everyone else. If a teenager enjoys working with younger children, someone will undoubtedly find out and encourage the teen to volunteer in the nursery or a children's outreach. If a young woman plays guitar, she is likely to be called upon to help with worship now and then. And when circumstances dictate that young people rub shoulders with people in different life stages, wonderful things can happen.

One small-church pastor I spoke to recently had this to say about this trend:

> We've been doing intergenerational ministry *a la fuerza,* as we say in Spanish—because we had no choice. I felt apologetic about this throughout the '80s and '90s, especially when we would lose families to the big churches that had the big programs for their children and youth. Imagine my surprise when at the turn of the century I started hearing

the big churches begin to verbalize their need in this respect and to name the value of keeping generations together instead of separating them at the parking lot!

As many churches are discovering, people of all ages benefit from the congregation's functioning as a family, particularly as people become ever more transient and move geographically farther from their biological families. Another group that benefits are those children or parents whose biological families do not share their faith. A mother of teenagers in our church recently told me that she depends on an elderly couple in our congregation to serve as grandparents to her children, because neither her parents nor her husband's are Christians.

Finally, ongoing research suggests that intergenerational ministry may be the key to ensuring that our teens remain committed to the community of saints. Researcher and youth pastor Kara Powell has been tracking 400 newly graduated high school students through their first three years of college in her College Transition Project. Though her research is ongoing, she can say with confidence, "There is a strong link between kids' involvement in intergenerational relationships and worship and their staying in church after they graduate."[9] The intergenerational relationships Powell has observed include teens' relationships with older adults as well as with younger children in the church. "Teens should not only be the objects of ministry," she explains. "They need to be the subjects of ministry, as well."

This issue is sensitive and challenging, and there is much hard work to be done. I don't mean to suggest that it will be easy. But the good news is this: The small-membership church is the ideal place for these important intergenerational

8

relationships to occur. Larger churches must hire new staff-persons to accomplish what the small church can do with ease: take the radical step of recognizing that the church exists not only to serve the family, but ultimately to serve *as* family.

NEW FOCUS ON THE FAMILY

Of course, a church can't claim to have embraced intergenerational ministry simply because it has members of several generations all sitting in the same room on a Sunday morning. A church can be without age-specific programs and still fail to engage its youth and children. I can provide excellent examples of that sort of ministry from my own experience.

One of the first churches I served as pulpit supply was a tiny congregation in rural southern Arkansas. The town was literally a bend in the road—Highway 7 to be exact. In that bend was a long-defunct gas station where something like an old Ford Torino stood up on concrete blocks. That Torino may well have been the station's last customer back in the mid-1970s, when the car was new.

The church building itself may have held fifty people at one time, but we never tested the seating capacity. Week after week, we had the same few worshipers: the elderly matriarch and her brother ("the deacon"); her two sons and their children. We were a three-generation church.

The family always sat together on the same pew to my right. The elderly deacon would sleep through the sermon. Afterward he would shake my hand and tell me, with bleary eyes, how lovely the message was. The grown boys would let their children play tag around the sanctuary—*while I preached*—until I became visibly distracted. Then they would bend the children over their knees and spank them—*while I preached*—for interrupting the service. This was not healthy intergenerational ministry.

Fortunately, positive examples of strategically small churches committed to intergenerational ministry abound.

A small Presbyterian church near Los Angeles has added elements of intergenerational service and mentoring to their catechism process. In order to convince the elder board and congregation that they have made the faith their own and are committed to church membership, teens must participate in a service project with a multigenerational team, attend a Bible study with older church members, and be involved in ministry to younger children. In this way, the church hopes to instill in its teens that faithful Christian commitment involves learning and serving as a family of faith.

Other churches are making more modest forays into intergenerational ministry. My church, for example, encourages the integration of adults in its Sunday school program. Instead of offering groups based on age or stage of life, our classes are attended by everyone eighteen years and older. I have found this arrangement quite rewarding. Having twenty-year-olds and eighty-year-olds discuss Scripture, current events, and the Christian life together makes everyone's experience richer.

We are also experimenting with integrating our children into the main Sunday worship service. At present, children from three years old through fourth grade leave the service just before the sermon to continue a more age-appropriate worship service in their own space. But in the summer, the children remain in the sanctuary the entire time. To help them engage in the adult worship, our minister of education (my wife) prepares worship folders that explain the elements of our liturgy, including a bulletin in a larger font (which is easier for new readers to follow), and provides a list of key words or phrases the kids can expect to hear that Sunday. During the months while the children are in the service, the adults regularly sing a few of the songs the children sing in their separate worship service.

We also have recently overhauled the children's Sunday school program in a way that encourages a greater number of intergenerational relationships. Before, we followed a very traditional format in which every grade and age group met separately with a single Sunday school teacher. Now all children from first through sixth grade begin every Sunday school hour together in a large group. There they sing a few songs together, hear a story from the Bible, and enjoy a drama of some sort (related to the story) performed by youth and adults. After this large-group time, they break into smaller grade- and age-specific groups. Class themes rotate every six weeks, so that the youth and adults who read and perform the Bible stories only commit to six weeks at a time. This arrangement is great for our kids, because they benefit from the large-group time with each other before they go into their smaller groups (and in our small church, there are only one or two children in some grades). But this model also allows a greater number of youth and adults to form relationships with the children of the church.[10]

Kara Powell insists that the smallest of steps toward intergenerational relationships within the church can make a significant difference. Ultimately, though, the onus for the success of intergenerational ministry rests on the older members of the congregations. They must embrace their potential as mentors, as functional parents and grandparents. This may feel awkward as first, as if they are overstepping their bounds. But the younger people will welcome the genuine interest of potential mentors, even if they are not likely to invite themselves into your care.

To clarify, I am not arguing that there is no place in the church for age-specific ministries. There are developmental concerns to consider in the education of children, youth, and even young adults. It is important that each of these age groups develop meaningful peer relationships. Teenagers in particular are going through life changes and have questions they may not feel comfortable asking in the presence of their parents or grandparents. As one student told his youth pastor, "I don't want to talk about sex with Grandma in the room." What I'm advocating is that we add to our age-specific programming a concerted effort to foster relationships across generational lines.

I should also acknowledge that intergenerational ministry is not easy and it might be costly. Even if a church's leadership decides that age-integrated ministry is healthy and effective, there are still parents and church hunters to convince.

Despite the difficulties, learning to understand the church as family will be profoundly rewarding. In fact, I am convinced that if the small church had no other inherent value, no other particular strength, this one thing would make it a strategic tool for the future of the Christian faith.

Questions for Reflection for Pastors or Leadership Teams

1. What opportunities do people have in your church to form relationships with people of other generations?

How might you be more intentional about these opportunities so that you make the most of them?

2. There are many ways to bring the generations together—in worship, service, education, or recreation. Which of these ways (or others) might be easiest in your church? Which could be hardest? Why?

3. Make a list of several people in your congregation who you think might be interested in forming deeper intergenerational relationships. Try to think of people from several age groups. How might you encourage these people to lead the congregation in integrating the generations?

Chapter Seven

Filling the Leadership Gap:
The Training Church

In February 2008, the blog *Out of Ur* moderated a heated debate after it featured comments from Eddie Johnson, the lead pastor of Cumberland Church in Nashville, Tennessee. What sparked the controversy was the language Johnson used to describe the relationship between his congregation in Nashville and North Point Community Church in metro Atlanta.

"Just like a Chick-fil-A," he explained, "my church is a franchise, and I proudly serve as the local owner/operator."

Franchise is an odd word to describe a local church, and owner/operator an unusual metaphor for the pastorate. But to Johnson, the designations make perfect sense. The appeal of a franchise—whether a grocery store, chain restaurant, or auto parts store—is that consumers know what to expect from their favorite brands at any number of locations around the world.

A latte from a Starbucks in Tallahassee should taste just like a latte from a Starbucks in Chicago or Seattle or Salzburg.

That's why Johnson is thrilled to be associated with the Atlanta church's "brand" as a satellite affiliate. People familiar with North Point will know exactly what to expect when they attend his "franchise" in Nashville. And they won't be disappointed. On most Sundays, the morning teaching at Cumberland is delivered via satellite video by the pastor of North Point Atlanta himself: the inimitable Andy Stanley.

The relationship between Cumberland Church and North Point Community Church is an example of a growing trend in large-church ministry. In most cases the remote locations are overseen by a site pastor who provides spiritual care for the congregation. These sites typically provide their own worship team, youth and children's ministries, and other standard programming. The mother church provides the sermon via satellite or video recording.

It's no wonder large churches find this technology appealing. Video venues and other remote location solutions play to the major strength of big churches, which are typically led by larger-than-life charismatic speakers. Sermon broadcast, of whatever form, allows large churches to extend their ministry reach even further by planting remote sites in neighboring cities, other states, and even other countries. Living Hope Church in Vancouver, Washington, for example, has twenty-three satellite campuses, including four international sites in New Zealand, India, Mexico, and the Philippines.[1] Best of all, these churches can do all this with just one gifted preacher. There's no need to find, develop, or send a qualified speaker to each location. They can simply send pixels.

Some ministry leaders argue that the video-venue strategy is a great opportunity for small congregations, as well, because one of the small church's greatest perceived weaknesses is their inability to attract or keep high caliber speakers.[2] With remote-location technology, any number of small churches can benefit from the preaching of a single exceptional speaker at the same time. This is exactly what Eddie Johnson finds so attractive about his church's relationship with North Point Community Church.

The trouble is, while the video-venue model plays to the key strengths of large churches, it actually undermines one of the key advantages of small congregations. Small churches have a better way of extending their ministry reach than hitching their wagon to a preaching star. They may not attract celebrity preachers, but they have the unique opportunity to develop and send out gifted leaders.

ABLE TO TEACH

The Evergreen Community in Portland, Oregon, is a strategically small church committed to reaching the lost in the notoriously pagan Pacific Northwest. By some estimates, only 1 percent of Portland's population is "religious," and that figure includes everyone from Buddhists and Hindus to Muslims and Christians. Because they minister in an environment that is hostile to religion, Evergreen has chosen to adopt somewhat unconventional tactics. One of those is intentionally remaining small. Relationships are critical for reaching religious skeptics, so the worship gatherings have to remain small enough to be intimate and interactive. Another is finding a safe meeting location. Right now Evergreen uses pubs. It seems a natural place to hold services in a city with the nation's highest number of microbreweries per capita.

Because Evergreen is committed to remaining small, growth in numbers poses a potential problem. The church has already outgrown a couple of pubs and reached the point where the only possible solution is dividing the congregation into multiple sites. Of course, multiple sites require multiple preachers. Which brings us to another core commitment at Evergreen: The heartbeat of the church's growth strategy is leadership development.

For the first few years of their existence, Evergreen benefited in its leadership team from pastoral staff and volunteers who had been trained by other churches. "At this point, that's not going to cut it for us anymore," says founding pastor Bob Hyatt. Now the church is seeing potential in people who began their Christian journey at Evergreen—people with no previous church experience—and Hyatt wants to transition them into leadership. For these people, "it takes more than simply saying, 'I think you've got what it takes to be a pastor, and I want you to help me.' The church needs a focused strategy for developing leaders."

The place where Evergreen's commitment to leader development is most evident is on the preaching schedule. The church has seven elders, and all of them preach on a regular basis. Bob is the main teaching elder at the church's first location, and there is a primary teaching elder at the other location. But all seven elders are on the schedule at both locations. The primary reason for this is theological. Evergreen is committed to the biblical qualifications for eldership, as they understand them. Among other character traits and qualities Paul makes requisite for elders, he says that they must be "able to teach" (1 Timothy 3:2; 2 Timothy 2:24).

But having all the church's elders preach regularly also serves a practical function. "Many advocates of video venues say there simply aren't enough church planters and talented teachers to go around," Bob explains. "And my response is that in a video venue world, *there never will be*." The only way to nurture other church planters and pastors is to give them experience. And that means giving them the pulpit.

There are risks, to be sure. Hyatt acknowledges that some of Evergreen's elders are more gifted in preaching than others. The congregation has endured its share of poor sermons (what congregation hasn't?). It should be said, though, that Bob doesn't consider a person for eldership if the church's leadership doesn't think they possess the gift of teaching at some level. Even so, they don't have to have celebrity potential. This means that Evergreen looks for different traits in potential elders. According to Bob, they "look for people who are already doing the work of an elder." When considering potential teachers from within their congregation, Evergreen's leadership is concerned first with a person's relationship with Jesus and general character. Then they ask these questions: "Who do people go to for advice and counsel? Who demonstrates the presence of wisdom? Who is already teaching others in some way?" Their approach enables them to achieve their greater goal: "The church isn't driven by a single personality, and several people are developing preaching experience at once."

This approach to leadership development would be impossible in most large churches. The risk is simply too great. Eddie Johnson, whom we met early in the chapter, was optimistic about the success of his church in Nashville because it could feature the preaching of Andy Stanley. If people come to his church on Sunday morning to hear an exceptional sermon from a celebrity preacher, they would be quite disappointed to hear a mediocre message delivered by a volunteer elder in training. A church focused on aggregating large numbers of people with attention-grabbing messages can't afford to put an amateur in the pulpit. Frankly, this puts them at a disadvantage, because someday that celebrity preacher will retire. It will be very difficult to find a suitable replacement.

Perhaps more important, Evergreen's strategy is kingdom focused, because it is organized to perpetually reproduce church leaders. The tendency of the American church to rely on exceptional preachers discourages leadership development. Bob Hyatt observes, "Pursued as a large-scale strategy, video venues will inevitably lead to fewer and fewer gifted and experienced lay and vocational preachers." The same can be said not only of video venues, but of all leadership models based primarily on the gifting of a single leader. The challenge, of course, is that our congregations have high expectations for their pastors' preaching. Rethinking the role of preaching in leadership requires significant changes in the way we think about the work of the church.

THE SUPREMACY OF PREACHING?

I never relished hospital visitation or officiating funerals or making evangelistic visits to the friends of church members. But the only pastoral duty that prompted anxiety dreams for me was preaching.

When I was preaching every week, I was a full-time student and had a part-time job. So as many busy pastors do, I often put off sermon preparation until Friday or Saturday. One night I dreamed that I had decided to forego preparation altogether. I'd just wing it on Sunday morning and hope nobody noticed. In my dream, it was just moments before the service, and I was on the front row organizing my thoughts. I brainstormed throughout the singing and took the pulpit fairly confident I could pull this off. But when I turned around and looked out over the congregation, my heart sank. There in the pews (which, of course, were filled to capacity) was every ministry mentor of my life, past and present. My hometown pastor and youth minister were there; so were my biblical studies and ministry professors, and a few random family members. They were all bright with expectation, and I was scared to death. I woke up a moment later in a cold sweat and worked on my sermon till morning.

I deserved a little anxiety for my procrastination. But most pastors I know feel considerable pressure to preach well, because many of their churches have essentially reduced the entire pastoral role to sermon delivery. Yes, congregations expect their pastors to visit and invest time in the staff and make an appearance at all the Sunday school parties. But they can be forgiven for doing these things poorly. Preach a bad sermon, however, and you'll hear about it for weeks.

Because we put so much emphasis on the preaching event, it can be easy to think that the primary way we lead and influence our congregations is from the pulpit, making preaching almost synonymous with leadership in some church circles. Congregations often reinforce this idea by the way they address or refer to their ministers. I don't know how many times someone took me by the arm and said, "I've got a question for you, *preacher*."

And because pastors and their congregations think of ministers primarily as preachers, pastors know they better preach well. Referencing the parable of the talents in Matthew 25, Darrin Patrick, lead pastor of The Journey in St. Louis,

Missouri, articulates what most of us suspect is true: "Whether we like it or not, believers and unbelievers are attracted to those with five- or ten-talent teaching gifts and are drawn to attend churches with that level of teaching." Because this is the case, pastors can feel that the weight of their church's success (typically measured by numbers in attendance) rests entirely on their abilities in the pulpit. After all, Darrin continues, "The larger the church the more talents the pastor is likely to have in the area of teaching."[3]

Darrin doesn't mean to imply that "pastors who only have two-talent teaching gifts aren't as important or godly." But that's how it feels. When I preached weekly, I would work hard to prepare my sermon, deliver it, and then afterward a well-meaning congregant would pull me aside and say, "I heard (insert name of celebrity preacher here) preach that same passage once, and he did it this way . . ." At least one of my deacons listened to sermon tapes every week—and not even from a celebrity pastor, but from the pastor of a church in the next town. It's no testimony to my skill that I left the congregation hungry for even two-talent preaching.

This is one of the pastor's greatest sources of insecurity. He can look out on his middling congregation and assume that the reason his church hasn't grown is because he isn't good enough. What a terrible weight to bear, when the success or failure of a congregation hangs on an event that occurs one hour per week and no more than fifty-two times per year.

Darrin accurately identifies the problem. But he fails to offer us a good solution. Probably because he is a gifted speaker himself, he believes relying on the ten-talent preacher is a legitimate approach to ministry. "Down through church history God has seemed pleased to use the teaching gift to draw large crowds and many of those people to himself," he explains. Again, he has hit upon a truth. But is this the way things were meant to be?

FINDING OUR STORY

The history of Christianity in America is often told as a genealogy of one exceptional preacher after another. That lineage typically begins with Jonathan Edwards, whose infamous sermon "Sinners in the Hands of an Angry God" is said to have left people clutching pew backs, white-knuckled and weeping for the salvation of their souls. From there we tell of George Whitefield, whose itinerate preaching ministry peaked when the young preacher was only twenty-six years old. (Sort of makes you sick, doesn't it?) Whitefield, it is said, could preach to nearly 30,000 without amplification and could send listeners swooning with his stirring pronunciation of the word *Mesopotamia.* We speak of John Wesley, who brought revival from atop tree stumps, and Charles Finney, who perfected the art of conversion, and Billy Sunday and Charles Spurgeon and Aimee Semple McPherson. Then we crescendo in the twentieth-century with Billy Graham, and we all wonder if there will be another national preacher like him.

As we listen to this story of God's work, we two-talent preachers wonder where we fit in the narrative. It's paralyzing to stand in the pulpit with an open Bible when you suspect that God works primarily through men and women like the ones listed above. It's not easy for the typical pastor to find comfort in history.

Fortunately, the Bible tells a different story, one we are more likely to resonate with.

Moses and the apostle Paul were arguably the two most important messengers in the Bible, excluding Jesus, of course. It's not surprising, then, that there are remarkable parallels between the prince of Egypt and the apostle to the Gentiles.

God called Moses to form a people out of slavery, the people of Israel. And in order to do that, he issued them a founding document—the Law—of which Moses was the privileged messenger. Paul, too, was called to found a people, the new Israel. They were made up of both Jews and Gentiles and were slaves in their own right to sin and darkness. To found this people, God entrusted Paul with another Word, the gospel, which he called the law of Christ.

Remarkably, neither of them were ten-talent preachers.

Moses, the Bible tells us, spoke with some sort of impediment. He assumed (he hoped, frankly) that his lack of polish would get him out of returning to Egypt to lead the Israelites to freedom. "O Lord, I have never been eloquent," he pleaded, "neither in the past nor since you have spoken to your servant. I am slow of speech and tongue." It didn't work. God found a way to work within Moses' weakness.

The apostle Paul is a somewhat more complicated example. He was accused by some critics of being an unimpressive preacher, in spite of the fact that his letters packed a punch (2 Corinthians 10:10). Yet we know that Paul was a persuasive speaker. He pleased the Athenians well enough that they wanted to hear more from him, even though they thought his message about resurrection was ridiculous (Acts 17:32). When he spoke to the Jews, he was often "arguing persuasively about the kingdom of God" (Acts 19:8).

When he was with the Corinthians, though, his approach

was different. Paul describes his preaching in Corinth in this way:

> When I came to you, brothers, I did not come with eloquence or superior wisdom as I proclaimed to you the testimony about God. For I resolved to know nothing while I was with you except Jesus Christ and him crucified. I came to you in weakness and fear, and with much trembling. My message and my preaching were not with wise and persuasive words, but with a demonstration of the Spirit's power, so that your faith might not rest on men's wisdom, but on God's power. (1 Corinthians 2:1–5)

I suspect that Paul could have preached powerfully among the Corinthians. He was a trained Pharisee and an educated Roman citizen. His preparation would no doubt have made him a formidable debater. But Paul probably suspected how much the Corinthians would appreciate a stirring speech and an eloquent turn of phrase and therefore, ironically, he took a different tack. It's likely that Paul knew what Darrin Patrick and you and I all know: People want to hear the ten-talent preacher. It's equally likely that for this reason precisely he stripped his presentation down to the basics, lest his listeners be charmed by the messenger and fail to hear the message.

In any case, Moses and Paul both understood that there was more to their carrying out God's purposes, more to being a shepherd of God's people, than the excellent delivery of a message one hour per week. Every pastor knows that one reason our sermons are often not as polished as we might like is because sermon preparation is only one item on a long list of weekly responsibilities. We could dedicate another chapter to the inestimable value of pastoral duties such as officiating baptism and

Communion, visiting the ill and homebound, sitting with a family in their grief, celebrating with congregants in their joy, and committing our brothers and sisters to the grave to await the resurrection. This is the ministry of presence—of simply being an ambassador of Christ to his people. This ministry may well be the most important role a pastor plays among his flock.

And truth be told, it is in these situations that much spiritual education actually takes place. The time a church leader spends on a parishioner's sofa or beside a hospital bed is likely to have a greater long-term effect than any single sermon he will ever preach. It is here that people ask difficult questions and pastors forgo easy answers. Here leaders preach sermons without a pulpit. And I suspect these sermons are better remembered.

In light of all this, it seems to me that our expectations of preaching come more from our national narrative than from the biblical one. The preaching of the Word of God is crucial to the health of a church. But we have so elevated the art and craft of preaching that we've diminished the importance of the many other functions of the pastor, functions in which the Word of God is present and active no less than in the pulpit. It's no wonder, then, that in a recent survey, the Leadership Network asked over two hundred mega-church pastors what they do best. Only 1 percent listed visiting members as their primary strength. Seven percent listed evangelizing and 10 percent pastoral counseling and spiritual direction. Nearly 80 percent said they were best at preaching and teaching.

Churches that see preaching as the pastor's primary function imagine the pulpit as the place where a single individual can exercise his or her gift for the edification of the entire congregation. The pulpit is the symbol of influence and control, and the only person who can fill it is the one with the greatest gift for public speaking. In a strategically small church, however, the pulpit can be a place where people not only exercise their gifts, but where they can develop them, as well. Perhaps then we can begin to measure success not by how many people show up to hear the preaching, but by how many people we are sending into the world equipped to serve as pastors.

TRAINING TEACHERS

For a congregation to function like Evergreen Community, it must shift away from the assumption that the pulpit is the place from which one gifted person ministers to a passive congregation and instead embrace the idea that teaching can be something the whole congregation can do. This value doesn't have to lead to something as radical as a seven-member preaching team. It simply means that a church begins to perceive the pulpit as the place to discover and edify fledgling leaders.

The first church I served had a strong sense of congregational calling. The small, rural congregation believed that they had been called to encourage and equip young pastors. Historically, most of their pastors had been college students, so they knew they probably would never keep the same pastor for long. The truth is, they didn't need to. They had a wise and gentle deacon that was for all intents and purposes the church's pastor. They let me make mistakes and endured terrible sermons. They gently corrected me when I used language the older folks considered inappropriate in church. Some Sundays, the head deacon would put his hand on my shoulder after the sermon and look at me with a smile that communicated "There's always next week." Every member was not so gracious, to be sure. There was one cantankerous old soul who told me after my very last sermon in the church, as we walked to my farewell potluck, that I used the pronoun *you* too often. "Makes it sound like you've got everything figured out and you're preaching down to us," he said. I thought a good many things but only said "Thank you."

On the whole, that experience was invaluable for me. The church did not consider the pulpit a place exclusively for a ten-talent preacher but as a place where the congregation could prove its commitment to developing leaders. I remain active in ministry to this day as a result.

Moreover, when a church conceives of the preaching of the Word as a responsibility and privilege that can be shared by multiple people, they might be surprised by how many gifted individuals their congregation contains.

A couple of years ago, the church I attend now was in the middle of a nearly two-year-long pastoral search. During that time, pastoral care and the majority of the preaching was done by an interim, a long-time church member who had served as a pastor in a previous phase of life. While the pastoral search committee was looking outside the church for a long-term pastor, our interim looked inside for gifted people to preach the Word.

The lectionary provided our text each Sunday, and at least a couple of Sundays a month our congregation provided a different preacher. It was a blessing to hear from so many of our own members. The congregation benefited from the diversity of perspectives in the pulpit each week. And the speakers themselves benefited, as well. A few young people with pastoral gifts and a sense of calling had an opportunity to hone their abilities and seek confirmation from the congregation that they should, in fact, pursue vocational ministry. Others had no interest in or calling to vocational service, but they were gifted communicators and brought challenge and encouragement to their fellow congregants. They even asked me to preach. Things had gotten desperate.

In our denomination, the pastor wears a black robe to symbolize that the person preaching is far less significant than the Word of God. Having new people in the pulpit communicates much the same thing. That year and a half was powerful for our church because our interim understood that we didn't need to hear from a ten-talent preacher every week. We needed to hear the gospel preached from members of our own congregation. In the process, several leaders emerged who have played important roles in our church ever since.

THE SUPREMACY OF SENDING

As has been the case with each topic we've addressed in this book, the primary question a congregation must ask is how to gauge the success of its ministry. Many churches will consider themselves successful if they have a polished and charismatic pastor who draws a crowd with his exceptional preaching. These churches typically measure success in terms of growth in congregation size. A great preacher brings in new people and may be more likely to retain the old ones, but this strategy may only be successful in the short term. A single charismatic leader leaves an enormous vacuum when he or she leaves the stage. It is very difficult for a protégé, no matter how talented, to live up to the expectations of his predecessor. Focusing on church attendance may well yield results for a season, but pouring energy into the raising up of elders and teachers can still bring increase long after the current pastor has retired. The equation changes from a matter of addition to multiplication. The initial investment may be higher and more demanding, but there is no limit to the payoff over time.

Because of this, strategically small churches like Evergreen measure success in terms of sending. The question is not "How many people are we attracting?" but "How many people are we calling, training, and sending?" In Matthew 9:37–38, Jesus tells his disciples, "The harvest is plentiful but the workers are few. Ask the Lord of the harvest, therefore, to send out workers into his harvest field." It is easy for a small church to be discouraged that it lacks a ten-talent preacher. But really, this is an opportunity in disguise: a chance to join Jesus in his mission and help empower workers for the harvest.

Questions for Reflection for Pastors or Leadership Teams

1. How do you currently identify and develop leaders within your congregation?

2. The Evergreen Community sees preaching and teaching as important aspects of the role of elder. Would your church consider adjusting its expectations of elders to include preaching and teaching?

3. Make a list of people in your congregation in whom you perceive leadership talents and gifting. Would you be willing to share the pulpit with them to help them develop their gifts? Would your congregation support such a decision?

Chapter Eight

Catch the Vision

My goal in writing this book has been to cast a vision for a new way of measuring success in our ministries. I have avoided offering systematic strategies and methodologies for making your church strategically small because the process will no doubt be different in every congregation. But the time for the hard work of application is fast upon us.

As I said at the beginning of our time together, the primary disadvantage of the small church isn't our methodology. Neither is it our location, our worship style, or our lack of resources. Our primary problem is perception. Many of us have been trained so thoroughly to imagine ministry success in a particular way, or according to particular criteria, that we've become disenchanted with our own churches. We can't strategize our way out of that mess. What we need is a

renewed imagination. I've tried to introduce you to a handful of pastors and churches that have become comfortable in
their small-church skin. My hope has been that if we could
just silence the experts for a few hours, we might have the time
and imagination to begin thinking about our ministries in
a new way.

In every chapter so far, I have given examples of churches
doing just that. I've called these churches *strategically small*
not because they are small on purpose (for the most part),
but because they recognize that being a smaller congregation
has its benefits. More to the point, they are putting those
benefits, that hidden potential, to good use. These churches
recognize that running a small church as if it were a big one
undermines the smaller congregation's key strengths. In a
culture, even a Christian culture, that values size, celebrity,
and institutional visibility, these strategically small churches
are underreported and underappreciated. Hearing their stories has renewed my hope in the future of the church, and the
small church in particular. I hope their examples have done
the same for you.

We've identified several unique strengths that the small
congregation has to offer. They are authentic and nimble.
They have everything they need to empower the laity for the
work of ministry, to facilitate and celebrate intergenerational
relationships, and to develop and deploy new leaders. The
churches we've encountered in these pages have learned to
leverage these strengths to great advantage. As a result, we
have seen what a small church can do when it stops thinking
of itself as a failed effort to get big and starts capitalizing on
its own unique strengths.

In this chapter, I'd like to offer a final example of a

strategically small church that embodies all of the strengths we've discussed in these pages. It's not just one church; it's a movement of sorts. More than anything else, it illustrates the shift in values that is necessary for a small church to become strategically small. For many of us, this will be a rigorous exercise for the imagination.

CHURCH IN THE Y

A few years ago, Antioch Church began holding services at the Countryside YMCA in Lebanon, Ohio, a northern suburb of Cincinnati. As many churches do, the congregation initially considered the location a temporary space that would suffice until they could find or build a permanent facility. But it didn't take long for Antioch to recognize the YMCA as a mission field in itself. Now the church has made this rented space its permanent home.

In the New Testament, the church went where the people were, explains Antioch's pastor David Newman. Today the Y is where people are. "I have several thousand people a day walking the halls in the place where I minister," David says. "That's an extraordinary opportunity."

To reach these folks, Antioch meets in a gym in the YMCA facility, for which they are charged a very modest fee. But what is truly unique about Antioch's vision and ministry is that they do not simply think of the Y as a meeting place. The majority of their outreach and ministry efforts are targeted in the Y with the goal of carrying the gospel to its many members.

Leadership journal published Antioch's story in the summer of 2008. Since then, a number of pastors have caught David's vision for seeing a church planted in every YMCA worldwide—all 14,000 of them. One of those pastors was Greg Douglas. In the spring of 2009, Greg and his wife were sent as ambassadors from their home church to plant a church in a YMCA in a neighboring state. Greg considers himself a missionary in the Y, so he began his plant much like a missionary would. He started by building relationships, becoming familiar with the organization's culture and values, and investing himself fully in the local branch, its members, and staff. The better he knows the people he ministers with and to, the more effective his ministry becomes.

The way David and Greg understand their ministries creates an inspiring vision that incorporates all the qualities of strategically small churches that we have addressed so far.

Reimagining Ministry Success

Whether they are planting a new church (like Greg) or moving an existing congregation into a YMCA (like David), being a Y church means rejecting a number of standard indicators of ministry success.

The first and most obvious has to do with the building. Few things validate a church's significance like having its own facility. My church met in a local community college for over a decade while it saved enough money to purchase land and build the building we meet in today. The church did remarkable ministry for the ten years it rented space. But moving into a permanent space that had our name on the deed (and mortgage) made the congregation feel somehow more legitimate. This feeling is natural, I think, and not unhealthy.

The Y church pastors, on the other hand, have decided not to measure success in terms of a permanent building of their own. They've found that committing to rent space long term has its own advantages. "The facility issue is the 800-pound gorilla on the church planter's back," Greg Douglas says. "What's great about the Y is that it's a ready-made church building—complete with worship space, Sunday school classrooms, rest rooms, and program space." Renting has a financial advantage, as well. David Newman explains, "I never change a light bulb, vacuum the floor, pay an electric bill, or worry about taxes. I couldn't pay half a janitor's salary with what the Y costs us in rent per year."

Ultimately, though, practical considerations are not what make the Y attractive for these pastors. More important to Greg and David is the fact that saving money in the cost of facilities frees finances to be used for the church's mission. Sacrificing a permanent building—with its mortgage, maintenance, and operating costs—may not look like success, but it gives the congregations greater resources for kingdom impact. Greg and David think in terms of kingdom growth rather than institutional growth.

The Authentic Church

Because each local chapter is relatively autonomous, the Y in every community can tailor its programming to best meet the needs of its neighbors, whether in an upper-middle class community or the very poorest of the inner city. Overseas, some YMCA branches operate homeless shelters, orphanages, and other significant social services (this must have been the sort of Y the Village People had in mind). In all locations, the members of a given YMCA represent a wide cross-section of the local population.

This makes the Y a strategic location for a church that is committed to authenticity. As we discussed in an earlier chapter, most large churches attract members from across a large geographical area. Instead of being deeply implanted in any one local community, they appeal to and extract a specific demographic from many locations. This works against a church's authenticity, as such a congregation can feel a bit like a franchise or chain. But because the Y is committed to serving neighborhoods instead of target demographics, they attract a diverse membership and are thoroughly local. By focusing its energies in and on the Y, churches that meet in a YMCA prove their commitment to strengthening the local community. What they sacrifice by renting space, they more than make up for in authenticity. They may never be able to provide professionally performed worship services (after all, gymnasiums are not known for their great acoustics), but genuineness attracts people who would never attend a more traditional church.

The Nimble Church

Families are often attracted to the Y by some desire for personal improvement, whether it's learning a skill, getting into shape, or spending more time with the kids. The YMCA designs its programming to help families accomplish these goals. A strategically small church that meets in a Y can invest its volunteer time and energy into this diverse programming while keeping its own programming lean and nimble.

Between Sundays, members of David Newman's Antioch Church teach classes; serve on the board; coach T-ball, soccer, and swim lessons—whatever they can do to be a missional presence at the YMCA. Greg Douglas, of Work of Christ Church, reports that focusing outreach efforts on the Y has helped his church focus its own vision for programming. In his conversations with Y personnel, Greg discovered that the branch was losing members because the staff was often unable to provide child care for children between eight and twelve years old. They simply couldn't find enough volunteers. In response, Work of Christ Church now provides volunteers for child care in that age group, which meets the Y's needs and gives church members an opportunity to form relationships with children and their parents from the community.

The Equipping Church

David and Greg are committed to equipping their congregants to minister from their passions. And they have a broad perspective on what types of activities constitute ministry. Everything from coaching a sports team or leading an after-school program to teaching a personal finance seminar can be ministry, if you recognize how God can be at work in the process. And because many of their members enter the church through Y programs, the pastors recognize the value of these activities and encourage their people to stay involved in them.

The Intergenerational Church

"The great thing about the Y," Greg says, "is that it's necessarily multiethnic and intergenerational." This is good news for the strategically small church committed to intergenerational relationships. Such relationships can be formed through the Y's existing activities, including sports and after-school educational programming.

The Training Church

Almost as a necessary consequence of its other commitments, the church in the Y movement is committed to leadership development. YMCA facilities offer only limited space, which makes perpetual numeric growth impossible. Each congregation can be only so big. Instead of basing success on the continual growth of one congregation, the Y church movement is based on the principle of multiplication. They don't want to see bigger churches; they want to see more churches—one in every YMCA.

At present, this training is taking place at the congregational level and through a series of videos on the Internet, which are aimed at awakening church planters and pastors to the opportunity of embedding a worshiping community in the local YMCA. Ultimately, though, the methods are unimportant. What's significant is the commitment to multiplication that drives Y church pastors to find, equip, and send more pastors into the field.

MINISTRY IN ABUNDANCE

A final characteristic of strategically small churches is that they do their ministry in a spirit of abundance.

The purpose of marketing is to create a sense of scarcity in consumers. Television commercials, Internet ads, and highway billboards are intended to make us feel as if our lives are incomplete without the products they advertise. Unfortunately, this same spirit pervades the church through the resources publishers and other "experts" market to pastors and church leaders. We are told that without the most current methodology or the latest technology, we are destined to obscurity.

As a result, many ministries operate out of a sense of scarcity. Before we ever begin, we feel a deficit of resources, staff, experience, volunteer support, or insight. Our vision for future ministry is often laden with if-onlys—if only we had more money; if only we had more staff; if only we had more opportunities.

At its worst, this attitude is a denial of God's provision. After all, Jesus instructed his disciples:

Therefore I tell you, do not worry about your life, what you will eat or drink; or about your body, what you will wear. Is not life more important than food, and the body more important than clothes? Look at the birds of the air; they do not sow or reap or store away in barns, and yet your heavenly Father feeds them. Are you not much more valuable than they? Who of you by worrying can add a single hour to his life?

And why do you worry about clothes? See how the lilies of the field grow. They do not labor or spin. Yet I tell you that not even Solomon in all his splendor was dressed like one of these. If that is how God clothes the grass of the field, which is here today and tomorrow is thrown into the fire, will he not much more clothe you, O you of little faith?

So do not worry, saying, "What shall we eat?" or "What shall we drink?" or "What shall we wear?" For the pagans run after all these things, and your heavenly Father knows that you need them. But seek first his kingdom and his righteousness, and all these things will be given to you as well. Therefore do not worry about tomorrow, for tomorrow will worry about itself. Each day has enough trouble of its own. (Matthew 6:25–34)

Church leaders remind their congregants of this great promise in their personal lives. But we are quick to forget that this promise extends to Christ's church, as well, and we end up doing our work in a spirit of scarcity. We are always keenly aware of what we lack. But Christ knows what his churches need. And if we trust that he gives us what we need, we can minister from a sense of abundance.

For example, if the majority of our ministry comes from programs imposed from the top down that require volunteer labor to be successful, we will almost certainly never have enough. We will always need twelve volunteers when we only have ten. But if we limit the number of programs we run and allow the rest of our internal and external ministry to arise as we equip people to serve where they are, then we will always be operating from abundance. Instead of lacking the support to run a few key programs, we will have ambassadors in innumerable initiatives. Instead of fretting about where we'll find enough support to meet our agendas, we will marvel at how God faithfully accomplishes his own.

If we think we can fulfill our calling to make disciples only when we can provide exciting worship and fellowship experiences for children, youth, and young adults, we will always be keenly aware of how we lack the space, talent, and leadership to make those things happen. If, however, we recognize that young people desire mentoring relationships above almost anything else, we can begin to see our congregation as a treasure trove of experienced Christians who are eager to shape the spiritual lives of young people.

If we are convinced that the purposes of God will only be accomplished when we have a celebrity preacher in the pulpit, then we will always operate in a spirit of scarcity. But if we put our hand to forming new leaders, new workers for the harvest, we will find ourselves in the spirit of abundance. Bob Hyatt of the Evergreen Community puts it this way: "What if instead of asking, 'Can he preach as well as me?' you ask, 'Can he or she, with a team of others, lead a Christ-centered community that starts small and grows, reproducing itself before becoming unmanageable and outgrowing the gifting of its leadership?' You might find more gifted and qualified people than you dreamed."

The question of scarcity and abundance relates to another theme we've returned to in the course of this book: cooperation and competition. I've suggested that most churches compete unintentionally, when (for example) they are unaware of what other churches are doing in their neighborhood. But sometimes competition can also be part of a church's ministry strategy.

The argument goes like this: In our capitalist economy, competition is good for consumers. When one company runs the show—whether a utilities or insurance provider, retailer, or grocery store—that organization has very little incentive to provide quality goods or services at a low price. They can charge whatever they want and produce a poor product or give sloppy service and it doesn't much matter. People have to buy their groceries someplace. When you add a little competition to the mix, however, companies have to step up to the plate. They can't assume that people will come to them, because other businesses are now providing better products at a lower price.

Some writers have suggested that the law of competition is as true for churches as it is for businesses.[1] Competition helps keep churches at the top of their game. When they have no competition in their neighborhood, churches can grow lax and comfortable. They might let their programming become tired and out-of-date. They may no longer care whether they are meeting people's needs. Competition may be a zero-sum game for churches—if one wins, another loses, but it's great for the people looking for churches, for "religious consumers."

You can probably guess how I feel about this way of thinking. The church's God-given job description is to make disciples, not to attract consumers. At the end of the day, every gospel-focused church is on the same mission—to see God's kingdom advanced on earth. Competition dilutes this mission, for it moves the focus off of Christ and his work and onto our ability to draw a crowd. And in the end it leads to ministry in scarcity. If we're ahead, we'll never be comfortable with our margin of victory. If we're behind, we'll be more concerned with catching up than with developing disciples. In either case, we'll focus too much attention on what we lack. Competition breeds scarcity and death. Cooperation, on the other hand, brings abundance and life. Together we can do more than we could do alone.

Just this summer our church partnered with five other churches in our town to provide school supplies for children who live in a low-income neighborhood nearby. Many of the apartments in the area are Section 8 government housing, and many of the families lack the resources to provide for their kids the things they need for school. This, in turn, puts a lot of pressure on the local school district, whose budget is already tight.

Throughout the summer, each of the churches involved collected supplies for a specified grade. (We were in charge of second graders, I believe.) On the Friday afternoon before school started in the fall, volunteers from every church met at our building to put all their supplies into backpacks that had been donated by yet another couple of area churches. By the end of the day, these volunteers had filled enough backpacks for 150 underprivileged elementary students.

The next day, the six churches hosted a block party in the target neighborhood. One church brought games for families to play together, another brought face painting and sports supplies. One provided tables and chairs. Each of the Anglo churches brought hot dogs and buns; one Latino church provided tacos (which were much better than our hot dogs). Representatives from the police and fire departments came and allowed children to tour the police cruisers and fire engines. As they played games and ate lunch, families of schoolchildren were invited to pick up their kids' school supplies. Together our churches ministered to nearly 150 children and their families.

Our church of about 300 is one of the largest in the city's ministerial association. There is no church in town large enough to have done all this alone. Together these six churches in Warrenville, Illinois, brought a taste of God's love and life to a needy neighborhood. In the end, it cost each church very little—every congregation brought school supplies, food, and chipped in around $100 for portable-toilet rentals and other related expenses. But the rewards are immeasurable. In terms of ministry strategy, this kind of participation opens the door for further collaboration. This is indeed ministry in abundance.

CONCLUSION: PREPARING YOUR HEART AND MIND

Many of the examples in this book require a new way of thinking that runs counter to the world's metrics for measuring value and success. Our culture encourages self-promotion. How else will we get the recognition we deserve? The church leaders and congregations in this book, on the other hand, often diminish themselves by staying behind the scenes. Our culture values the accumulation of power and influence. But throughout this book we've met pastors and leaders who consciously and carefully distribute authority and control to others. In other words, humility is an important characteristic of the strategically small church. Certainly many big-church pastors are humble, and many small-church pastors are not. But it should be clear by now that leading a strategically small church requires a renovation of the heart and renewing of the mind even more than new strategies and methods.

When you finish reading this book, I invite you to lay it on your desk or in your lap, pause briefly, and try to see your church as it is. Forget what the experts say you must have to make an impact. Consider what you have. What are your church's strengths? What are you doing already? What can you jettison? What programs can you kill? Who in your congregation is a leader just waiting to be developed, a lay minister waiting to be empowered? Don't make a list. Not yet. Just look and wait and let the Holy Spirit give you the insight to imagine ministry in abundance that can transform your church from "just small" to strategically small.

Notes

CHAPTER ONE

1. Henri Nouwen, *In the Name of Jesus: Reflections on Christian Leadership* (New York: The Crossroad Publishing Company, 2002), 56.
2. Perry Noble, live from the *Unleash* conference in March 2009.
3. Dietrich Bonhoeffer, *Life Together* (NY: HarperCollins, 1978), 27–28.
4. Ibid.

CHAPTER TWO

1. James Long, "Dave Gibbons," *Outreach* (May/June 2009): 84.
2. Alan Hirsch, *The Forgotten Ways: Reactivating the Missional Church* (Grand Rapids: Brazos Press, 2007), 31.
3. Greg L. Hawkins and Cally Parkinson, *REVEAL*, 33.
4. Neil Cole, *Organic Church: Growing Faith Where Life Happens* (San Francisco: Jossey-Bass, 2005), 9.
5. "The Axis Avalanche," *WILLOW* magazine (Sept./Oct. 2001).
6. Collin Hansen, "The X Factor," *Leadership* (Summer 2009): 27–28.
7. Rita Healy, "Why Home Churches Are Filling Up," *Time* (February 27, 2006).

CHAPTER THREE

1. James Gilmore and Joseph Pine, *Authenticity* (Boston: Harvard Business School Publishing, 2007).
2. Dan Kimball, *They Like Jesus but Not the Church: Insights from Emerging Generations* (Grand Rapids: Zondervan, 2007), 37.
3. Ed Stetzer, Richie Stanley, and Jason Hayes, *Lost and Found: The Younger Unchurched and the Churches that Reach Them* (Nashville: Broadman & Holman, 2009), 197.
4. Kimball, 214.

CHAPTER FOUR

1. Alex Cohen, "Nonprofit News Web Site Wins Coveted Media Award," *All Things Considered*, National Public Radio, npr.org (April 7, 2009).
2. Reggie McNeal, *The Present Future: Six Tough Questions for the Church* (San Francisco: Jossey-Bass, 2003), 24–25.
3. Andy Stanley in "State of the Art," an interview with *Leadership* (Spring 2006): 27.
4. For a great discussion of this topic, check out Skye Jethani, *The Divine Commodity: Discovering a Faith Beyond Consumer Christianity* (Grand Rapids: Zondervan, 2009).
5. Eugene Peterson, "Embracing the Church God Gave Me," *Best Advice: Wisdom on Ministry from 30 Leading Pastors and Preachers*, ed., William J. Carl III (Louisville: Westminster John Knox Press, 2009), 130.
6. Chuck Coward's article "One King's Money, Another King's Men," *Leadership* (Summer 2008), offers some great perspective on this issue. *www.christianitytoday.com/le/2008/summer/13.41.html*.

CHAPTER FIVE

1. Tom Sine, "Small Wonders," *Leadership* (Fall 2008).
2. "CNCS Releases 'Volunteering in America' report," National Conference on Citizenship, *www.ncoc.net/index.php?tray=content_blog&tid=&cid=2gp38*.
3. Alan Hirsch, "Defining Missional," *Leadership* (Fall 2008): 20.

CHAPTER SIX

1. Available at *www.americanreligionsurvey-aris.org/reports/ARIS_Report_2008.pdf.*

2. Thom S. Rainer and Sam S. Rainer, *Essential Church? Reclaiming a Generation of Dropouts* (Nashville: Broadman & Holman, 2008), 2.

3. Christian Smith, *Soul Searching: The Religious and Spiritual Lives of American Teenagers* (Oxford: Oxford University Press, 2005).

4. Rainer & Rainer, 4.

5. "The 100 Best TV Shows of All Time," *Time* (August 13, 2007).

6. Stetzer, *et al., Lost and Found,* 129.

7. Cynthia Long Westfall, "Family in the Gospels and Acts," in *Family in the Bible* (Grand Rapids: Baker Academic, 2003), 136.

8. Diana R. Garland, *Family Ministry: A Comprehensive Guide* (Downers Grove: InterVarsity Press, 1999), 320.

9. Kara Powell, "Is the Era of Age Segregation Over?" *Leadership* (Summer 2009): 45.

10. We use the *Jubilation Station* curriculum developed by Scottie Mae and published by Cook Ministry Resources.

CHAPTER SEVEN

1. Alexandra Alter, "Inspired by Starbucks," *The Wall Street Journal* (June 13, 2008), *http://online.wsj.com/article/SB121331198629268975.html.*

2. One example is Lyle Schaller, *Small Congregation, Big Potential: Ministry in the Small Membership Church* (Nashville: Abingdon Press, 2003).

3. Darrin Patrick, "Equal Time on Video Venues," *Next-Wave E-zine* (October 2006).

CHAPTER EIGHT

1. One example is Lyle E. Schaller, *From Cooperation to Competition* (Nashville: Abingdon Press, 2006).

BRANDON J. O'BRIEN is a doctoral student in historical theology at Trinity Evangelical Divinity School (Deerfield, Illinois) and editor-at-large for *Leadership* journal. He has served as pastor of two small, rural congregations, and now serves as a deacon at his church in Warrenville, Illinois, where his wife, Amy, is minister of Christian education. Brandon's writing has appeared in *Leadership, Christianity Today, Relevant,* and *Neue*. Find out more about Brandon at his Web site, *brandonjobrien.com*.

Acknowledgments

It takes a lot of support to turn an idea into a book. Marshall Shelley encouraged me to pursue the opportunity to write this book. The experience has been invaluable, and I would have missed it were it not for Marshall's urging. Several people deserve credit for making this book better. Drew Dyck and David Swanson read every chapter. Both men are fine writers themselves, and David is a pastor of a small church, so their input and observations were invaluable. My old friend Michael Cox and my new friend Kara Powell both helped me think through the scriptural basis and practical implications of a particularly difficult chapter. Their expertise was a tremendous help, for which I am quite thankful. And my editor, Andy McGuire, patiently read and reread multiple drafts of this manuscript. These fine folks made the book better. It still has its deficiencies, but they are all my fault.

Other friends and colleagues provided less direct, though no less crucial, support. My dear friends Brian Lowery and Skye Jethani helped me talk through every chapter before, during, and even after writing. I'm sure they are glad the book is finished. Of course, I am particularly indebted to the pastors and church leaders I interviewed while writing. I won't name them here because I credit them in the book. To all of you, it was a joy hearing your stories and an honor sharing them with others.

Finally, I couldn't have pulled this off without the support of my wife, Amy. She patiently listened as I talked about small-church ministry over meals, in the car, and everywhere, sharpening my thoughts and keeping my feet on the ground. She also pulled double duty at home while I spent my energy writing. To her and everyone else who made this possible: I consider this an accomplishment for all of us. Grace and peace to you in abundance.